Infant/Toddler Caregiving

A Guide to

Routines

Second Edition

Janet Gonzalez-Mena

Developed collaboratively by the

California Department of Education
and WestEd

the Program for infant toddler caregivers

Publishing Information

Infant/Toddler Caregiving: A Guide to Routines (Second edition) was developed collaboratively by the Child Development Division, California Department of Education, and the Center for Child and Family Studies, WestEd. (See Acknowledgments on page x for the names of those who made significant contributions to this document.)

This guide was edited by Faye Ong and Allison Smith, working in cooperation with Sheila Signer and Peter Mangione of WestEd and Mary Smithberger, Consultant, Child Development Division. It was designed and prepared for printing by the staff of CDE Press, with the cover and interior design created and prepared by Paul Lee. Typesetting was done by Jamie Contreras and Carey Johnson. It was published by the Department of Education, 721 Capitol Mall, Sacramento, California (mailing address: P.O. Box 944272, Sacramento, CA 94244-2720). It was distributed under the provisions of the Library Distribution Act and *Government Code* Section 11096.

© 2002 by the California Department of Education
All rights reserved

ISBN 0-8011-1510-8

Ordering Information

Copies of this publication are available for $12.50 each, plus shipping and handling charges. California residents are charged sales tax. Orders may be sent to the California Department of Education, CDE Press, Sales Office, P.O. Box 271, Sacramento, CA 95812-0271; FAX (916) 323-0823. See pages 158 through 160 for complete information on payment, including credit card purchases, and an order blank. Prices on all publications are subject to change.

Other resources on the Program for Infant/Toddler Caregivers available from the Department appear on page 157. In addition, an illustrated *Educational Resources Catalog* describing publications, videos, and other instructional media available from the Department can be obtained without charge by writing to the address given above or by calling the Sales Office at (916) 445-1260 or 1-800-995-4099.

Photo Credits

The California Department of Education gratefully acknowledges Fern Tiger and Associates for the use of the photo at the bottom of page 56; WestEd for the use of the photographs on pages 31 and 127 from the video *Room at the Table* and the photographs on pages 39, 114, and 132 from the video *The Next Step: Including the Infant in the Curriculum;* and Sheila Signer, Consultant, WestEd, for the use of the other photographs that appear in this document.

Notice

The guidance in *Infant/Toddler Caregiving: A Guide to Routines* (Second edition) is not binding on local educational agencies or other entities. Except for the statutes, regulations, and court decisions that are referenced herein, the document is exemplary, and compliance with it is not mandatory. (See *Education Code* Section 33308.5.)

Prepared for publication
by CSEA members.

Contents

A Message from the State Superintendent of Public Instruction

No issue is of greater concern to families today than obtaining high-quality child care for their children. Despite the critical need for quality child care, often such care is extremely difficult to find, particularly for infants and toddlers. As a result, the California Department of Education has made it a high priority to help develop programs that have safe, healthy, and intellectually engaging child care environments with warm, dedicated, and well-trained staffs.

The California Department of Education and WestEd's Center for Child and Family Studies joined forces to develop the Program for Infant/Toddler Caregivers, a comprehensive and innovative training system for child care providers in both centers and family child care homes. The program consists of caregiving guides, videotapes, trainers' manuals, and training institutes to help caregivers provide quality care for infants and toddlers. These materials are now being used throughout the world, reaching tens of thousands of caregivers in California, the United States, and internationally.

This document, *A Guide to Routines*, is one part of these materials designed to improve the quality of infant/toddler child care. The information and ideas presented in it focus on daily routine care for infants and toddlers. The guide illustrates the importance of keeping the emphasis on the child as you carry out caregiving routines throughout the day. It also covers diverse issues, such as promoting health and safety, caring for children with special needs, and being responsive to families.

Thank you for your interest in building strong child care programs, and I hope you find this guide to be a useful resource. You are doing a very important job for the youngest members of our society—our infants and toddlers.

DELAINE EASTIN
State Superintendent of Public Instruction

Preface

At a time when half the mothers in the United States are gainfully employed, most of them full time, more young children require care outside the home than ever before. The growth of child care services has failed to keep pace with the rapidly increasing demand, making appropriate care for young children difficult for families to find. Training is needed to increase the number of quality child care programs, yet the traditional systems for training child care providers are overburdened. In response to the crisis, the California Department of Education's Child Development Division and WestEd have developed an innovative and comprehensive approach to training infant and toddler caregivers called The Program for Infant/Toddler Caregivers. The Program is a comprehensive training system consisting of a series of training videotapes, caregiver guides, and trainer's manuals.

The purpose of the caregiver guides is to offer information based on current theory, research, and practice to caregivers in both centers and family child care homes. Each guide addresses an area of infant development and care, covering major issues of concern and related practical considerations. The guides are intended to be used hand in hand with the program's series of videos: the videos illustrate key concepts and caregiving techniques for a specific area of care, and the guides provide extensive and in-depth coverage of a topic.

This guide was written by Janet Gonzalez-Mena, an expert in the area of routines in infant/toddler care. Like the other guides in the series, this one is rich in practical guidelines and suggestions. The information and ideas presented in the document focus on how the daily routines of caring for infants and toddlers can become opportunities for promoting the child's learning and development as well as deepening the relationship between child and caregiver. Special attention is given to such topics as parents' concerns, the need for consistency between home and child care, and cultural diversity in child care programs.

KATHY B. LEWIS
Deputy Superintendent
Child, Youth, and Family Services Branch

MICHAEL JETT
Director
Child Development Division

About the Author

*J*anet Gonzalez-Mena is a writer, consultant in early childhood education, and former community college instructor with experience as an early childhood education practitioner. She taught preschool and directed several child care programs, including an infant/toddler program, a family child care network, and a program of therapeutic day care for abused and neglected children.

Ms. Gonzalez-Mena is the author of several college textbooks on early childhood education, including *Infants, Toddlers, and Caregivers,* with Dianne W. Eyer. In addition, she has written a number of articles for *Young Children*, the journal of the National Association for the Education of Young Children. The articles include "What's Good for Babies?" and "Toddlers: What Are They Like?"

Ms. Gonzalez-Mena has also written about parenting. Her article for *Child Care Information Exchange,* "Mrs. Godzilla Takes on the Child Development Experts," argues that parents should not try to model themselves after preschool teachers. Instead, parents should accept and love that part of themselves which is not perfect, especially with respect to their child-rearing behavior. Ms. Gonzalez-Mena also writes about cross-cultural and multicultural perspectives in early childhood education.

Ms. Gonzalez-Mena has a Master of Arts degree in human development from Pacific Oaks College. Infants have been an important part of her life, as she has raised five children of her own and has been studying the field of infant/toddler caregiving for the last 25 years. She credits much of her knowledge and excitement about early child development and care to Magda Gerber. Ms. Gerber's philosophy of respect for infants has strengthened Ms. Gonzalez-Mena's own convictions about the importance of treating each child, no matter how small, as a full human being.

Acknowledgments

The first edition of this publication was developed by the Center for Child and Family Studies, WestEd, under the direction of J. Ronald Lally. Special thanks go to Ruth T. (Toby) Gross, M.D., for her contributions to sections of this document; Peter L. Mangione, Carol Young-Holt, Janet Poole, and Sheila Signer, content consultants, WestEd; Kathleen Bertolucci, WestEd, for editorial assistance; and Mary Smithberger and Kathryn Swabel, Consultants, Child Development Division, California Department of Education, for their review and recommendations on content. Thanks are also extended to the members of the national and California review panels for their comments and suggestions. The national panel members were T. Berry Brazelton, Laura Dittmann, Richard Fiene, Magda Gerber, Asa Hilliard, Alice Honig, Jeree Pawl, Sally Provence, Eleanor Szanton, Yolanda Torres, Bernice Weissbourd, and Donna Wittmer. The California panel members were Dorlene Clayton, Dee Cuney, Ronda Garcia, Jacquelyne Jackson, Lee McKay, Janet Nielsen, Pearlene Reese, Maria Ruiz, June Sale, Patty Siegel, and Lenore Thompson.

This second edition offers expanded information on issues of cultural sensitivity and conforms with current exemplary child care health and safety practices. It reflects, but does not match, the revised program standards for Head Start. Author Janet Gonzalez-Mena and Sheila Signer, Project Manager and Editor, wrote new sections or modified them under the direction of J. Ronald Lally, Director of the Program for Infant/Toddler Caregivers. Peter L. Mangione and Janet Poole of WestEd and Mary Smithberger of the California Department of Education, Child Development Division, reviewed and made recommendations on the content. Special thanks are due to consultants Karen Sokal-Gutierrez, M.D., M.P.H.; Sally Ashbach, R.N.; and Marsha Sherman, Director, Child Care Health Project, for their review of health and safety issues. Denise Eshabarr, Administrative Assistant, Center for Child and Family Studies, WestEd, provided editorial assistance.

Introduction

Why have a whole guide on caregiving routines? How hard is it to give a baby a bottle, change a diaper, put on a sweater? The question is not how hard or easy it is to engage in caregiving but how to do it in such a way that both children and caregivers benefit from and find pleasure in the contact. What might otherwise be a chore or drudgery becomes an opportunity for interaction and learning. A cycle can be established in which the caregiver sees the child's pleasure and satisfaction as evidence of a job well done and feels appreciated. The child's participation in the routine leads to both cognitive and emotional discoveries. The purpose of this guide is to help caregivers find ways to carry out routines that are enjoyable and convenient to themselves as well as good for the child.

Routines should be anything but routine except in the sense that they happen over and over. Instead of putting yourself on automatic pilot and getting the job done, you should view these special times every day as opportunities to interact with each child on a one-to-one basis. Each routine, no matter how often performed, should be a spontaneous event every time. Spontaneity will happen if you use those times to make real human contact—visual, verbal, and tactile. It will happen if you are sensitive to the child's responses and initiatives. It will happen if you

Caregivers are more apt to find satisfaction in caregiving routines when they pay attention to the whole child, not just to the immediate task.

are two people involved in a single task. It will not happen if you insensitively perform a procedure on a child or if you do the chore in order to get it over with.

The ideal is for the caregiver to use feeding, napping, and toileting or diapering routines as opportunities to build a close personal relationship with each child while attending to the child's individual physical, emotional, and developmental needs. This approach is good not only for the child but also for the caregivers who are more apt to find satisfaction in caregiving routines when they pay attention to the whole child, not just to the immediate task.

Well-carried-out routines are effective far beyond the single immediate goal. Anyone can give a baby a bottle. But giving a baby a bottle only satisfies an obvious and immediate need. The *way* in which you give the bottle makes the experience a full one. If you do the task sensitively and effectively, you can satisfy the baby's needs for attention, tactile stimulation (holding and touching), interaction, and attachment. You can enhance the baby's self-esteem, feelings of security, cognitive skills, and language skills.

Caregiving routines take up to 80 percent of a caregiver's time. The way in which these routines are carried out, day after day, has a major impact on young children. The caregiver's emotional tone, nonverbal messages, pace, and style of verbal communication, in addition to the actual content of the routine, need to be carefully considered.

Routines are the heart of infant/toddler care and a major part of the curriculum. During feeding, diapering, washing, and

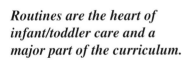

Routines are the heart of infant/toddler care and a major part of the curriculum.

dressing, the child learns many things not necessarily related to the specific lesson of the routine, such as:

- Security and self-esteem
- Pleasure and tactile stimulation
- A sense of time and space and rhythms
- Independence and competence
- Cognitive and language skills

Routines work better in a primary caregiver system in which each caregiver has the major responsibility for specific children. This system is preferable to one in which all caregivers share equal responsibility for the whole group. If the primary caregiver is the adult who usually feeds, changes, and toilet trains the child, the two get to know each other better than if all caregivers try to concentrate on all the children. For example, sensitive and consistent napping procedures with the same caregiver, whenever possible, make it easier for children to fall asleep and offer the opportunity for intimate, personal contact.

Effective caregiving responds to each child's developmental level. Routines for *young infants (birth to nine months)* are carried out in a consistent, gentle, and timely way so that the children learn basic trust in the world. They get used to having their needs met and come to anticipate the caregiver's response to their messages.

Routines for *mobile infants (six to eighteen months)* focus on the infants' increasing competencies as the children learn to feed themselves, toddle to the sink to wash their hands, and help pull up their pants. Caregivers sensitive to this age group know that mobile infants may resist being diapered, but caregivers regard this resistance in a positive light. Instead of taking the resistance personally, the caregivers know that mobile infants would rather be moving and exploring than lying still.

Routines for *older infants (sixteen to thirty-six months)* take into account the children's vacillation between independence and dependence. Older infants are likely to be quite cooperative one minute, helping to set the table, and run in the other direction the next minute when asked to hang up a coat. They may ask the caregiver to do a simple task they have been able to do for months, such as putting on a shoe, then turn around and try to tie it themselves even though the task is way beyond them.

There is no formula for performing caregiving routines. They must be carried out each time as an experience shared by two people rather than a procedure one person performs on another. Caregiving is a dynamic moment-to-moment activity.

Sensitive and consistent napping procedures with the same caregiver, whenever possible, make it easier for children to fall asleep and offer the opportunity for intimate, personal contact.

Information about what and how much should be done is not memorized from books but is learned each time in the interaction with the child.

Information about what and how much should be done is not memorized from books but is learned each time in the interaction with the child.

Information from the parent (or family representative) should also be a part of the picture. (See appendixes A and B for sample information forms.) Caregiving is easy when there is consistency between the way the caregiver does things and the parent's goals and expectations. In that case the caregiver can simply focus on the interaction with the infant during caregiving times. However, sometimes the parent has very different ideas about what should happen and how. Those ideas are often based on time-honored cultural and family practices and mean a great deal to the families involved. If the caregiver and parent have different opinions, they must talk to each other until each understands the point of view of the other and they can come to an agreement about how routines should be handled in the child care program.

Sometimes both parties agree that it is all right if what goes on in child care is different from what happens at home. They may see this as support for the child's adjustment to a bicultural world. However, caregivers who are not sufficiently acquainted with the culture of the family may make snap judgments about possible harm caused by the family's practices at home without understanding the parents' goals or beliefs.

Conversely, parents may feel the caregiver is insensitive to deeply held cultural values. They may think that their children are becoming disconnected from their culture and even from the family. This is a serious issue. Supporting family ties is an important part of the caregiver's role in promoting the infant's positive identity formation and development.

What kinds of value conflicts might arise? Independence versus interdependence is one example. The goals of independence and individuality are not shared by everyone, whether they live in the United States or in other countries. Some cultures downplay individuality and promote interdependence over independence, thereby fostering strong family ties, pooling family resources, and sharing the family home across generations. Learning about different values and points of view can help caregivers understand why a family's expectations of a child's development of independence, such as self-feeding, may be different from the objectives of the program. Such knowledge can prevent unnecessary misunderstandings and tensions.

Reminders are given throughout the guide about areas in which cultural conflicts may come up. If a conflict does arise, caregivers need to treat parents' concerns seriously and with respect; work to understand the parents' point of view; and incorporate the parents' desires, if possible. If not, they need to negotiate a mutually acceptable alternative.

This document is divided into separate sections on the individual caregiving routines, focusing on practical advice about how to conduct them. Every section addresses the three age groups: the *young infant (birth to nine months),* the *mobile infant (six to eighteen months),* and the *older infant (sixteen to thirty-six months).* Each section urges you to take full advantage of the opportunities in each routine for one-to-one interactions. Consistency between home and child care and in the child care program is a theme in each section. For convenience, the term used throughout the document to refer to the child's principal family caregiver will be "parent." However, it is understood that families come in many configurations and that the parenting role may be shared with or taken on by other relatives or non-relative caregivers.

The challenge is to take the information offered here and figure out how to fit it into your own unique style of caregiving as you work to meet the individual needs of each infant, toddler, and family. How can you carry out routines in ways that are beneficial to children and families yet convenient and pleasurable for you? How can you handle routines in ways that reflect your own personality—your unique way of dealing with the

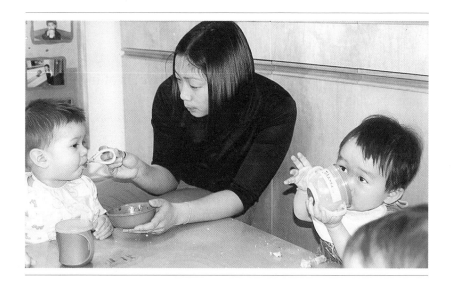

Learning about different values and points of view can help caregivers understand why a family's expectations of a child's development of independence, such as self-feeding, may be different from the objectives of the program.

world—and, at the same time, be responsive to families' cultural and lifestyle concerns?

The complexity of carrying out the routines of daily care with all these issues in mind clearly means that no recipes can be given in a book such as this one. Each routine must reflect what parents and caregivers have agreed is best and bring the child and caregiver together in a way that deepens their relationship. Thus, this document is offered as a *guide* to the creative and committed caregiver, not as a set of specific instructions on how to do caregiving routines.

Section One:
Greetings and Departures

Arrival and departure times are important in building relationships between the caregiver and parent (or family representative) and between the caregiver and the child. Separation anxiety on the part of the parent and the child may require sensitive handling. In addition, arrival and departure times are often the only regular opportunity for exchanging information between the caregiver and parent. As the child and parent make the sometimes difficult transition from home to child care and child care to home, the caregiver and the parent exchange information and strengthen their partnership of caring for the child.

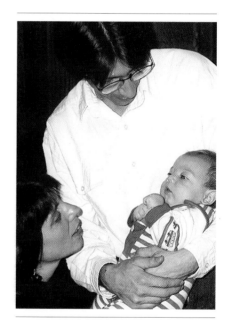

Arrival Routines

Arrivals are important because they can set the mood for the whole day. Skilled caregivers are able to greet both parent and child and make each feel welcome as well as exchange information, provide parents with child development information, and help both parent and child cope with feelings of separation. It is quite a feat for the caregiver to attend to all those concerns in a couple of hurried minutes and still keep an eye on the other children in his or her care. But the arrival routine can be done with sensitivity to child and parent—and is being done so on a regular basis by thousands of caregivers every day.

Information Exchange

It is important for the caregiver to learn from the parent how the child slept and ate, the child's mood, the state of his or her health, and family events that could influence the child. Because infants and toddlers cannot explain very well what they are experiencing, caregivers need all the pertinent information the parent has. In that way the caregiver can combine the knowledge with

Through the regular exchange of information, problems surface, giving the chance for both caregiver enlightenment and parent education.

the child's signals in order to determine needs. Is the child crying from hunger, or is the child crying because he or she has been up since 4:30 a.m.? That is the sort of information parents can provide.

The caregiver can give the parent(s) information on what can be expected that day: "Sarah's friend Jesse is out sick today, so Sarah may feel less secure than she usually does." "Rebecca is bringing her new puppies in this afternoon. Is there a problem with fears or allergies that staff should watch out for?"

Parent Education

Through this regular exchange of information, problems surface. The exchange can provide not only caregiver enlightenment but also parent education. Perhaps a mother talks about how she is at her wit's end because her child has just learned how to climb out of the crib and now she cannot get the child to sleep at night. The caregiver can give the parent suggestions of books or articles to read, identify other parents who have recently conquered such a problem, describe how napping is handled in child care, or even invite the parent in to see how staff members handle sleep routines.

Of course the caregiver more than likely does not have a lot of time to talk with the parent. The parent's time is probably limited, and the caregiver needs to give some attention to the child. It is quite rare that caregivers talk privately to parents during arrival time. If the child is present during the information exchange (which is usually the case), the child should be included in the conversation in some way rather than be spoken of as though he or she were a piece of furniture. Try to give attention to both parent and child whenever possible.

Separation Techniques

Separations may vary greatly for parents and children, depending on circumstances ranging from the family's previous experience with child care to how tired the child is on that particular day. Parents of very young infants often experience painful emotions at this time, especially during the early stages of adjustment to group care. These emotions come from the natural and strong protective urges that adults of all species feel toward the young. However, knowing what to expect during various stages of child development can help caregivers and parents prepare for separations.

In the first months most children do not react to being left in child care. Although they respond differently to familiar people, most babies are accepting of strangers. When the child enters care as a young infant, the process usually goes smoothly, at least from the infant's point of view. The parent says good-bye to the baby and then hands him or her over to you. A baby younger than five months will rarely cry at separation.

A mobile infant may have more trouble separating from the parent. At about six months of age, infants begin to distinguish strangers and (sometimes) to fear them. By nine months of age, children may be going through what is called separation anxiety and may cry lustily at even the prospect of being left in child care.

As children get older, their understanding of separation deepens and the child's temperament, culture, and other factors may be

The separation may be as painful for the parent as for the child.

more important. An older infant may become involved in play while you are talking to the parent and may seem unconcerned about the impending separation. In that case, when it is time for the parent to leave, simply encourage him or her to say good-bye to the child and stand by for the child to come to you afterwards. Even a child who plays comfortably on his or her own while the parent is present may need reassurance when the parent leaves.

On the other hand the child may stay close to the parent the whole time, even clinging to the parent while you talk, and react strongly to the idea of separation. In general, it is best not to rush the child who is dealing with feelings about the separation. Having the parent stay for a while allows the child time to become more comfortable in the setting. Your attitude in this situation can convey a sense of security to both parent and child. Show that you care about the parent's and the child's feelings and, at the same time, show your confidence that the child will be fine. When the parent has gone, acknowledge the child's feelings, assure the child that the parent will return, and be prepared to spend some extra time comforting the child and supporting his or her adjustment to care.

During the early stages of your relationship with the child, it is often helpful to make indirect contact with the child. If the child seems fearful of you, avoid direct contact, even eye contact, and try interacting through a toy or another object of interest to the child. Set the toy down slightly away from you or place a barricade, such as a table or a basket of blocks, between you and the child.

This gives the child the message that you and the toy are available without overwhelming the child with your presence.

Help children cope with separation by:

Going slowly

Making good-bye a transition

Allowing a transition object (blanket, etc.)

Knowing what to expect from different ages

(The video *First Moves: Welcoming a Child to a New Caregiving Setting* shows clearly how to use this approach.)

Making good-bye a slow transition instead of a sudden break is useful unless prolonging the transition worsens it. At some point the best solution may be for the parent to say good-bye to a child who is anxious about the impending separation and allow the caregiver to deal with the child's feelings. In that case you need to get through the information exchange quickly, then try to ease both parent and child through the separation. Some children are comforted with a transitional object from home, such as a special blanket, a favorite stuffed animal, or even something of the mother's. Other children find objects in the child care setting that comfort them. Such objects should be available and offered if they help.

Caregivers are sometimes surprised when the child who has been left happily for weeks suddenly starts protesting when the parent says good-bye and starts out the door. This fear of separation is a perfectly normal stage of development and shows cognitive maturation as the child comes to understand more about how the world works. Knowledge of that developmental phase may be of some comfort to the caregiver who is left with a screaming baby trying to pry the door open to follow mother or father.

Finally, the caregiver's understanding of how the parent of the fearful or protesting child may be feeling is important. Some parents seem to suffer even more than their children. That emotion may result in ambivalent behavior as the parent feels torn between leaving and staying. If the parent has been having twinges of guilt about leaving the child, a display of separation anxiety on the part of the child may explode those twinges into overblown feelings with which the parent has trouble coping. Caregivers may need to spend time and effort comforting the parent and helping him or her move out the door. After the parent has left, further time and effort may be needed to help the child cope— although some children brighten up the minute the parent leaves.

Departure Routines

The end of the day may bring another surprising explosion of the parent's or child's feelings or both. Although many children greet their parents happily when they arrive in the afternoon, some children do not. An infant or toddler may be as matter-of-fact about mother's arrival as the child was about her departure in the morning. But that behavior may be disconcerting to the parent. If a parent is feeling a bit insecure about his or her relationship with the baby, a caregiver's well-meaning statement "He did just fine—he didn't even miss you" may tear the parent apart. The parent does not want to hear that the child suffered because of his or her absence, but the parent also does not want to hear that the child was not affected by it.

Not Wanting to Leave

Mobile infants and toddlers may be absorbed in what they are doing at the moment and may not give the attention to the parent's arrival that he or she expects. Or the child may have a particularly difficult time with transitions, with the result that he or she protests when it is time to leave. Such behavior can absolutely crush a parent. A sensitive caregiver can help the parent not to take it personally.

Then there are the children who are angry at being left in child care and who react to their parents by resisting going home at the end of the day. These children may ignore their parents or run in the other direction. Some children even cry and complain loudly. It is surprising but not unusual when children who complain at being left in the morning also complain about going home in the afternoon. Caregivers can assist with departures by letting children know in advance that soon they will be going home. "Mommy's going to be here soon. She's coming in her car to take you home, to see your baby sister and your auntie."

Feeling Deserted

The last children to be picked up may develop feelings of being deserted. It is not unusual to see a child's anxiety mount as more and more children depart before his or her parent arrives. Reassurance as well as some special attention from the caregiver is called for here.

While dealing with feelings in both the adult and the child, the caregiver also has some physical tasks, such as turning over the diaper bag, child's clothes, and so on. To keep the exchange simple, the caregiver should organize the child's belongings ahead of time. Involving the child in these departure routines can turn an anxious time into one of anticipation.

Exchanging Information

The caregiver also must be aware of the parent's needs. Almost everyone is tired by the end of the day, and hunger may

The last children to be picked up may develop feelings of being deserted.

*The parent needs to know
what went on that day*

be another factor. Somehow, in spite of all the potential difficulties, the caregiver must again exchange information with the parent. The parent needs to know what went on that day: specifics about naps, feedings, bowel movements, any symptoms of illness, and injuries that may have occurred. How the baby's day went, what happened, and what kind of moods he or she displayed are also of interest to parents. Of course, some positive words about behavior and accomplishments are always welcome and make the parent feel more a part of the child's daily life.

If the caregiver who works the late shift does not have all this information firsthand, it is important that he or she has access to the earlier caregivers' records and shares them with the parent. The records may be a combination of check sheets with facts (times, amounts, and so on) and a log of short anecdotes.

The caregiver should end the information exchange by adding a word or two about the following day to help maintain the bond: "See you tomorrow, Jessica. The puppies will be here again, and you can pet them."

Although arrival and departure times are transitions, they are vital to building relationships between parents and caregivers. The ongoing daily contact, brief though it may be, is when the caregivers and the parents get to know each other. The caregivers learn about the parents' approaches to child rearing as well as the parents' cultures, personalities, hopes, and fears. The ideal outcome of this relationship building is a spirit of teamwork as parent and caregiver work together in partnership for the good of the child.

Points to Consider

1. How can you make the social–emotional climate during arrivals and departures warm, friendly, caring, and personal?
2. When the parents say good-bye and walk out the door, what differences in behavior might you expect from a three-month-old, a nine-month-old, and a two-year-old? How can you respond sensitively and effectively to children in each of those age groups if they are having separation difficulties?
3. How can the routines of arrival and departure be positive learning experiences for the child and a valuable part of the curriculum?
4. How can arrival and departure routines be made convenient for the caregiver and meet the needs of the child and the parent?

Suggested Resources

Books and Articles

Culture and Childrearing. Edited by Ann L. Clark. Philadelphia: F. A. Davis Co., 1981.

Explores different cultural points of view on a variety of child-rearing topics, such as attachment to parents and separation.

Fraiberg, Selma H. *The Magic Years: Understanding and Handling the Problems of Early Childhood.* New York: Charles Scribner's Sons, 1984.

Offers practical information for caregivers on how to understand messages from babies and how to engage in a truly reciprocal relationship with infants.

Gerber, Magda, and Allan Johnson. *Your Self-Confident Baby: How to Encourage Your Child's Natural Abilities from the Very Start.* New York: John Wiley & Sons, 1998.

Presents Gerber's philosophy of respect for the autonomy and competence of infants and toddlers in relation to all aspects of care, including daily routines.

Gonzalez-Mena, Janet. *Multicultural Issues in Child Care* (Third edition). Mountain View, Calif.: Mayfield Publishing Co., 2001.

Explores cultural differences in beliefs, values, attitudes, approaches, and practices.

Gonzalez-Mena, Janet, and Dianne W. Eyer. *Infants, Toddlers, and Caregivers* (Fifth edition). Mountain View, Calif.: Mayfield Publishing Co., 2001.

Discusses how to respect children's feelings while helping them cope with situations such as separation.

Lally, J. R. "Feeling Good About Saying Goodbye," *Working Mother* (August 1985), 54–56.

Presents a practical approach on how to help a child adapt to a new caregiving setting. The suggestions can apply to any situation in which a caregiver helps a child make a transition.

Lane, Mary, and Sheila Signer. *Infant/Toddler Caregiving: A Guide to Creating Partnerships with Parents.* Sacramento: California Department of Education (with WestEd), 1990.

Explores issues and suggested approaches in relating to parents of infants and toddlers who are being introduced to a child care program. Examines in detail the meaning of separation for the parent as well as for the child.

Setting Up for Infant/Toddler Care: Guidelines for Centers and Family Child Care Homes (Revised edition). Edited by Annabelle Godwin and Lorraine Schrag. Washington, D.C.: National Association for the Education of Young Children, 1996.

Includes practical information regarding business aspects of setting up a child care program. Experts describe how to promote all areas of a child's development.

Audiovisuals

Babies Are People, Too. Los Angeles: Churchill Films, 1985. Videocassette or 16 mm film, color, 27 minutes; printed guide.

Focuses on the relationship between young mothers and their children during the first two years of life. Demonstrates techniques for smoother transitions from child care at the end of the day. Available from SVE & Churchill Media, 6677 No. Northwest Hwy., Chicago, IL 60631. Telephone: (800) 829-1900.

First Moves: Welcoming a Child to a New Caregiving Setting. Sacramento: California Department of Education (with WestEd), 1988. Videocassette, color, 26 minutes; printed guide.

Presents practical techniques caregivers can use to introduce young children to a new care setting and ease often difficult separations between the parent and the child.

Human Development: A New Look at the Infant—Attachment (Program 5). Irvine, Calif.: Concept Media, 1983. Videocassette or filmstrip/sound cassette, color, 27 minutes; printed guide.

Reviews Mary Ainsworth's work in the area of attachment. Discusses attachment behaviors and the role they play in separations and reunions. Explores the importance of caregiver sensitivity. Available from Concept Media, P.O. Box 19542, Irvine, CA 92713-9542.

Information Hotline

California Child Care Health Line: 1-800-333-3212

This hotline provides child care health and safety information Monday through Thursday, 8 a.m. to 4 p.m.

Section Two:
Feeding

Feeding is one of the most important activities in any infant/toddler program. Attention to the way the caregiver feeds children in his or her care can produce a wealth of benefits. The feeding process not only promotes physical development but may enhance cognitive and language development as well. Perhaps most important of all are the social and emotional experiences that come with feeding: feeding enhances attachment, increases feelings of security, and provides warmth, acceptance, and an overall sense of well-being. The video *It's Not Just Routine* demonstrates proper procedures for feeding (along with diapering and napping) and shows how the routine promotes learning and deepens attachment.

Communicating with Children

When a familiar caregiver takes a hungry young infant in his or her arms, the message should be, "I'm here for you. I care about you. I have time for you." When the caregiver sits with a

The more the home and the program can coordinate food and eating routines, the better.

mobile infant, patiently feeding that child cereal, allowing the child to explore and experiment with a hand or spoon, the message is the same. In addition, the caregiver is saying, "I value your curiosity, sensory needs, and growing independence." When the caregiver sits pleasantly with a group of older infants, helping them serve portions, talking about the food, replacing dropped spoons, and offering paper towels for spills, he or she is giving the message that mealtime is an important social time and that the children are capable, worthy human beings who are cared about. The video *Ingredients for a Good Start* is a good source of information about how children's food and feeding style needs are linked to their developmental stage.

Communicating with Parents

Caregivers' communication with parents about the feeding process is essential. The more the home and the program can coordinate food and eating routines, the better. Caregivers need to know about the child's dietary history and needs, schedules, habits, tastes, preferences, allergies, and sensitivities; they also need to convey to parents what was offered, what was consumed, and how the child received the food that day. (See Appendix C for a sample form.)

Records for young infants are fairly simple because most of their nutritional needs are met through breast milk or formula. For the parent's information, daily records should be kept of how much was consumed, when, and what solids were offered and consumed. For mobile infants, a record is still necessary, particularly as these children may be trying new foods. The parents need to know when new foods are served in case the food causes an adverse reaction, which can range from diarrhea to hives to emotional upset. For older infants, post menus of meals and snacks where parents can see the notices and keep some kind of individual record.

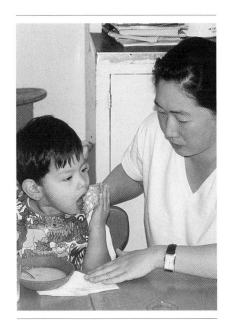

Individual, family, and cultural perspectives on food must be discovered and considered, even though accommodating the family's preferences may complicate the program. For example, if a child has a milk allergy or lactose intolerance, it is important that the child not be given milk; instead, give a substitute recommended by the health care provider and parents. If the family is vegetarian, it is important that the staff respects the meat restriction and finds other ways to ensure older infants get enough protein. Young infants get the protein they need from breast milk or formula, but after six months they need solid food. Beans and tofu are good sources of protein for vegetarian mobile and older infants.

If the family's cultural approach to infant nutrition differs from mainstream approaches, the caregiver should feed the child what he or she is used to, when feasible. The natural diet of most cultures is nutritionally sound, though some diets may seem strange and perhaps unbalanced. Learning about diets of other cultures can also be educational and personally interesting for caregivers.

Breast-feeding

Any mother who has an inclination to breast-feed should be helped to do so. The program that supports breast-feeding mothers provides a comfortable, quiet corner for them to be with their babies and minimizes interruptions during feeding. Of course, the caregivers do not make the decision, but they can do a lot to encourage breast-feeding.

Child care providers have an opportunity to make a significant contribution to infant health by supporting breast-feeding and the provision of mother's milk for infants in child care. The American Academy of Pediatrics now recognizes breast-feeding as the superior method of feeding babies under the age of six months. Unfortunately, in the United States, the rate of maternal breast-feeding has actually decreased over the last 20 years. A study by the American Academy of Pediatrics indicates that while most women who are planning to reenter the workforce after the birth of their babies intend to breast-feed, only 20 percent of them actually do so for longer than six weeks after they go back to work.

Although caregivers are not responsible for the failure of mothers to continue to breast-feed after working, caregivers *can* be instrumental in helping mothers to succeed. It is common knowledge that human breast milk is the "perfect food" for young babies and contains antibodies beneficial to the infant; therefore, caregivers should be knowledgeable about breast-feeding and equipped to support mothers in nourishing their babies.

Breast milk is a remarkable food for babies, especially for those in group care situations. The child receives antibodies that the mother has passed on through her milk. When a baby is exposed to germs and then breast-feeds, the breast produces the disease-specific antibodies to which the child has been exposed. This protection, in combination with the nutritional aspects of

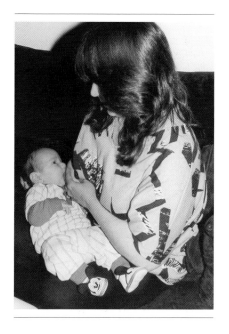

Individual, family, and cultural perspectives on food must be discovered and taken into consideration.

the milk, makes breast-feeding well worth any slight inconveniences to the mother or caregivers.[1]

Bottles

Babies who have been breast-fed from birth frequently do not know how to suck from an artificial nipple. They may turn their head and protest vigorously when offered a bottle even when hungry. When it is possible, a mother can express breast milk soon after the baby's birth and get someone else to feed the baby several times a week. This arrangement may still meet with resistance later on but will give the caregivers an extra edge in re-teaching the baby how to suck from a nipple. A first introduction to a bottle is usually best handled by someone other than the mother and is best received if the bottle contains breast milk.

A baby who is refusing to take a bottle can be induced to do so by a patient and persistent caregiver. Holding the bottle away from the body and turning the baby away from the caregiver, plus walking or movement, usually with a drowsy baby, can get the baby to suck and be rewarded without being confused that he or she is about to nurse. This technique may take several efforts to feed the baby daily for a week or more, so do not get discouraged. In the meantime liquid can be dribbled into the baby's mouth with a spoon if liquid intake is of concern. Babies may prefer one particular bottle or nipple to another. When trying to encourage a baby to take a bottle, offer several styles of bottles and nipples. Some babies have a decided preference for one style or another. The "orthodontic" style and "natural" style seem to work the best most of the time.

Storage and Preparation of Expressed Breast Milk

Mothers can express milk manually through hand, electric, or battery-operated pumps. Once expressed, the milk should be stored in glass or hard plastic containers (the process of warming the milk in disposable bags can release chemicals used in the production of the bag into the milk and, therefore, should not be used). This milk can be kept refrigerated for up to two days and frozen in a conventional freezer for up to two weeks; a zero-degree freezer offers even longer storage capacity.

Babies should be held for bottle-feeding and fed when hungry.

---

[1] Bobbie Edwards, Certified Breastfeeding Educator, contributed the information in this section, much of which comes from the Lactation Institute and which appeared in a slightly altered version in the document *Setting Up for Infant/Toddler Care.* Edited by Lorraine Schrag and Annabelle Godwin. Washington, D.C.: National Association for the Education of Young Children, 1993.

A bottle of milk or breast milk can be heated in a pot of warm (not boiling) water for five minutes or under a hot faucet to room or skin temperature. Shake the bottle to distribute the heat evenly because hot spots can cause burning. *Under no circumstances should any milk be warmed in a microwave oven.* Breast milk is relatively unstable and may lose its nutrients during the microwave process. Even more seriously, microwave heating continues after the oven has been turned off. Very young children can scald their throats when they drink the overheated milk from a bottle.

Support for Mothers

Mothers who choose to combine working and breast-feeding need much support and assistance. They may feel guilty because they have been unsuccessful at getting their baby to accept a bottle at home. They may be pressured at work not to take the time to express milk or not to leave the office in the middle of the day to feed their baby. A baby who is healthy and whose immune system can fight infections well has an advantage in any group care situation; therefore, it is to the caregiver's benefit as well as the baby's and mother's benefit to help a mother through these difficulties.

Mothers who are nursing have the additional complication that the hormones released during the breast-feeding process are also those that stimulate maternal feelings and can make it more difficult to separate from their child. Assuring the mother that her feelings are normal can help her through the process. Setting up a quiet place to feed the baby after a long day's work can help a mother make the transition from her professional life to her personal life as well as ease the guilt she may feel about the separation. Breast-feeding can be a peaceful and intimate reunion time for mother and baby.

Support for the Baby

Babies digest breast milk more easily than they do formula. Consequently, babies who are being breast-fed tend to need more frequent feedings than those who receive formula. Caregivers must respond to this need by offering smaller amounts more frequently. Keeping a bottle of water available may also help. If a baby appears to be hungry, and the mother is due to come and feed the baby within 45 minutes or so, a very small amount of warm water can stave off the hunger pangs without filling up the baby. Some mothers may choose to offer supplemental bottles of formula. If the baby refuses this option but is doing well with bottles in general, suggest that breast milk be mixed with the formula in gradually decreasing amounts until the baby accepts the formula.

Professional Services

Caregivers can assist breast-feeding mothers by keeping on hand the telephone numbers of local lactation consultants and referring mothers to those consultants when problems or difficulties arise. Lactation consultation is a fairly new profession that offers services in most areas. Consultants and breast-feeding educators are specially trained to help mothers with problems or difficulties associated with breast-feeding. They can give advice about milk expression, choices of breast pumps, sore breasts and nipples, engorgement, or the breast-feeding of babies with special needs. They are also trained to help a mother develop a special plan to succeed in breast-feeding while she is working. To find a lactation consultant, look in the local Yellow Pages Telephone Directory or consult area obstetricians. A local organization called La Leche League may also have sources for help and support.

Although combining breast-feeding and child care may take some additional effort and attention, it is well worth it to all parties involved. The feeling of satisfaction that a caregiver gets when seeing a healthy mother and baby together is beyond measure.

Bottle-feeding

Most young infants will be bottle-fed by caregivers, whether the bottles contain breast milk or formula. Even though bottle-fed, infants should receive the same personalized attention as the baby who is breast-fed by his or her own mother. Focused attention by a primary caregiver ensures that all babies will get both the right amount of food and emotional nurturing.

Healthy and safe bottle-feedings are important. Infants in child care should receive formula that is as similar as possible to what they receive at home. Young infants should always be held with their bottles; bottles should never be propped for feeding. Babies who drink from bottles and are lying down may choke and are also at risk of ear infections. Of course, glass should not be used for children's bottles, cups, or dishes for safety reasons. Plastic is most appropriate, and clear plastic is helpful for children's bottles and drinking glasses so both you and the child can see the liquid.

The mobile infant continues to need the focused attention of a primary caregiver while being bottle-fed. Mobile infants may be capable of holding the bottle, but it is still preferable for them to be held during the bottle-feeding if they are comfortable in the caregiver's arms. When mobile infants show a strong preference for having a bottle on their own, encourage them to recline on a pillow that elevates their heads while a caregiver is nearby.

Children who are left with bottles in their mouths for long periods may develop dental problems. Decay of the front teeth is a common problem with infants who are put in bed with their bottles or who walk around with them. Juice and other sugary substances in the bottle are not the only causes of baby-bottle tooth decay. Even milk in the child's mouth for an excessive time can lead to this problem. Baby-bottle tooth decay can create long-term dental problems well beyond the stage of baby teeth. Because of this the program policy should be: *Never put babies to bed with bottles or let them walk around with them.* The child who arrives in the program used to treating a bottle as a pacifier that can be carried around and played with may protest about not being allowed to do so. Share information about baby-bottle tooth decay with parents and ask them to consider adopting at home the program policy noted above. This will support the child's health and safety as well as help the child in adapting to child care practices.

The feeding schedule should be individualized for each infant and be flexible enough to accommodate the child's daily needs. Infants should be fed when hungry, not when the clock or schedule dictates. Consistent care is important in feeding infants. They need to be able to trust that, soon after they communicate hunger, they will be fed by a familiar caregiver who understands their signals and is in tune with them.

What does it mean to be an "in-tune" caregiver? In-tune caregivers read the baby's signals and respond appropriately. They can recognize the difference between a tired cry and a hungry one. They are sensitive to the baby at any given moment even when the baby is not crying. For example, when feeding a very young infant, caregivers soon realize that the baby cannot look and suck at the same time or listen and look and suck. In-tune caregivers are careful not to distract or entertain when the baby is hungrily eating, yet they are willing to play briefly when

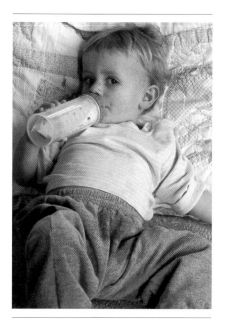

When mobile infants show a strong preference for having a bottle on their own, encourage them to recline on a pillow that elevates their heads while a caregiver is nearby.

the baby stops for a short time after taking the edge off his or her hunger and indicates an interest in the adult. In-tune caregivers know when to burp the baby, and they stop the feeding when the baby indicates he or she has had enough. The video *Getting in Tune: Creating Nurturing Relationships with Infants and Toddlers* explains this concept of reading signals and responding appropriately.

Weaning

As the child grows older and begins drinking from a cup and eating solid foods, the bottle takes on less nutritional importance. When a child can meet all his or her nutritional needs from eating solid food and drinking from a cup (usually when the child is around one year of age), the child may be weaned from the bottle. However, the decision of when to wean a child from breast feeding should be made on the basis of what works best for each mother and child. Ideas about and approaches to weaning are as strong and varied as those on starting solid food. Two approaches are described here.

Weaning can begin early on as a very gradual process by giving liquids other than formula or breast milk from a spoon, starting from the first weeks. As the child matures, a cup is introduced long before the child can hold it independently; he or she learns to drink with the adult holding the cup. As the child becomes a proficient drinker while holding the cup, the daily number of bottles or breast-feeding sessions is decreased gradually until he or she takes all liquids from a cup and no longer takes the bottle or breast. Some people who use this approach aim to

Ideas about and approaches to weaning are as strong and varied as those on starting solid food.

18

complete the weaning process about the end of the first year—when the infant no longer needs the bottle for nutrition and may become emotionally attached to it if the bottle is continued.

Another approach to weaning is not to worry about it or even plan for it but to let the child determine when to give up the bottle or breast. The cup is introduced at an appropriate age, but no attempt is made to cut down on bottles or breast-feedings. If the adult does not become impatient, the child "outgrows" the need, although the age at which this happens can vary greatly—from one year to as late as six years. In some cultures breast-feeding a six-year-old is acceptable.

More commonly, however, sometime before the child's second or third birthday, parents decide they have had enough of bottles or breast-feeding and stop. Usually that happens without too much trouble unless the child has a strong emotional attachment or the issue becomes a power struggle.

Abide by the parent's wishes, within reason, both in introducing solids and in weaning. You may have strong opinions, too, but they may not agree with those of the parent. Respect the parent's preferences, and when there is a critical difference of viewpoint or opinion, discuss it and negotiate with a parent.

Starting Solid Foods

Currently recommended practice suggests four to six months of age is the right time to start solid foods, depending on the needs of the individual infant. According to Mike Samuels and Nancy Samuels in *The Well Baby Book,* before children reach four months of age, "studies of stool samples show that most of the food passes through undigested. The young baby is not able to break down the complex molecules in many fats, carbohydrates, and protein."[2] In addition, feeding solids to very young infants can cause choking and increases the child's risk of developing digestive problems and food allergies. For personal or cultural reasons, parents have very different ideas about introducing solids. Some parents want their child to start eating solid food at a few weeks (sometimes reporting that the child seems to sleep better because the stomach stays full longer); others want to wait a year. Offering parents information about the risks of introducing solids too soon and, conversely, about the mobile infant's need for nutrients beyond those available in breast milk

Infants should be introduced to new foods gradually, one food at a time.

    [2] Mike Samuels and Nancy Samuels, *The Well Baby Book.* New York: Summit Books, 1979, p. 147.

or formula may influence their decisions about when to begin feeding the child solid foods.

When introducing a new food to infants and toddlers, take individual temperaments into consideration. Some children will take delight in each new experience whether it is a new food or a new toy. Those children relish novelty. Other children will be much more cautious about something new, and you will need to go more slowly with them. They are likely to spit out the first taste of a new food. Do not force them but keep trying. Be patient. Repeated exposure over a period of time is the key to success with the cautious child. The temperaments of infants and toddlers are important considerations in carrying out routines. The video *Flexible, Fearful, or Feisty: The Different Temperaments of Infants and Toddlers* presents more information about temperament and offers suggestions for caregiving.

Young Infants

Young infants should be introduced to new foods gradually, one food at a time. For example, you may offer one taste the first day, a spoonful the second day, and two spoonfuls the third day. Wait a week before giving a full serving. That way the child slowly gets used to the new flavor and texture; if he or she is allergic to the food, you will know which food is the cause so you can stop serving it before triggering a strong reaction.

Keep beginner foods simple. Do not add sugar, salt, or spices—infants appreciate the natural flavors of food without the additives most adults are so used to. Avoid serving children processed foods with artificial flavors or colors. It does not make sense to add complicated chemicals to a young system. Cereal, particularly infant rice cereal, is the most common food to start with. Moistened with formula or breast milk, the cereal can be as pasty or runny as you find effective for easy spoon-feeding. *Avoid the use of honey as a sweetener for infants under twelve months of age because of the risk of infant botulism.*

Be sure you are thoroughly acquainted with the parents' plan for introducing new foods and be as consistent with the home as possible. Parents or their pediatricians may have a particular order for new food introduction. Respect their preferences; some parents and pediatricians believe that if you introduce sweet foods such as strained fruits first, the child will resist less sweet food such as strained vegetables and meat. Other parents and pediatricians believe that the best method is to introduce fruits first because the sweetness is familiar to the child.

Most pediatricians advise delaying the introduction of certain foods until the infant is at least twelve months old. Infants are commonly allergic to foods such as egg white, orange juice and other citrus, cow's milk, and chocolate. Young infants (birth to nine months) and mobile infants (six to eighteen months) should not be fed fried or greasy foods in child care. It is important to promote the development of healthy eating habits and food preferences from an early age to prevent later problems, such as the build up of fatty deposits and high cholesterol. Carbonated and sugar-sweetened powdered drinks should also be avoided; they have no nutritional value and even reduce a child's appetite for more nutritious foods.

Be careful that the child can manage finger foods and will not choke.

Begin with strained foods and offer finger foods later, being careful that the child can manage the finger foods and will not choke on them. Anything with a hard or crunchy texture that can be bitten off but is difficult to chew is inappropriate for the young and the mobile infant. Avoid unpeeled apple slices and raw carrots. Even some soft or chewy foods may be dangerous. For example, hot dog rounds, marshmallows, peanut butter, and grapes have all been known to cause choking. Avoid them along with hard candy, nuts, raw peas, dried fruit, pretzels, chips, popcorn, and chunks of meat too large to be swallowed whole. If you see children being fed inappropriately, seek opportunities to respectfully share this information with families.

Be aware of each child's ability to swallow. Sometimes children with slight, even undetected neurological problems cannot coordinate chewing, swallowing, and breathing and will gag or choke easily. Often parents can tell you whether their children need special attention in this area. Be very cautious about what you give those children to eat, even when they are older infants and everyone else is having an easy time with the food.

Mobile and Older Infants

Mobile and older infants, who are no longer strictly dependent on breast milk or formula for nutrition, need a wider variety of foods—both those eaten with utensils and finger foods. However, even older infants should be restricted from foods such as popcorn, peanuts and other nuts, peanut butter, hot dog rounds, chunks of meat larger than half-inch cubes, and grapes because of the danger of choking. And older infants with any history of or inclination toward swallowing difficulties should be restricted to the soft, safe foods of young infants (see the video *Room at the Table* for information about feeding children with special needs).

Older infants may serve themselves and be encouraged not to take more than they can eat.

When you introduce a new food, take a positive attitude, as if you expect each child will like the food. If not all do, avoid reacting too strongly. You can suggest matter-of-factly that each child taste the new food, but do not insist that it be eaten. Also, do not get into a power struggle over the one taste. Older infants are known to change their minds easily if you do not make a fuss. The next time the food appears, they will probably try it and may even like it. Your responsibility ends at offering a balance of foods and feeding children unable to feed themselves.

It is not your responsibility to force children to eat certain foods or amounts of foods. Offer children a balanced diet, but let them determine what and how much they will eat. Provide a variety of nutritious foods: fruits, vegetables, whole grains in the form of cereals and breads, legumes such as peas and beans, dairy products, eggs, and meat. Over a period of time, children will select for themselves a balanced diet, even though they may make unbalanced choices on any given day.

Do not scold, punish, ridicule, or bribe children about what they eat or do not eat. (When you do that, you get out of tune with the child as the video *Getting in Tune: Creating Nurturing Relationships with Infants and Toddlers* shows.) Give small enough servings so that children can ask for seconds, thus stimulating appetites and minimizing waste. Older infants may serve themselves and be encouraged not to take more than they can eat.

It is important, however, to understand that in some families, self-service may not fit into the parents' ideas of good caregiving. And while the foods you serve older infants (sixteen

22

to thirty-six months) should be high in nutrients and low in fat, sugar, and salt, they should also reflect the children's cultures and accommodate their personal tastes as far as possible. Older infants, like young and mobile infants, need no additives in their foods—even additives such as salt, sugar, spices, or artificial colors or flavors. However, the children will have acquired a taste for the flavor of the food they are served at home; therefore, the foods served in the child care setting may not appeal to them at first and may, in fact, be in conflict with family or cultural tastes. It is worthwhile to help parents understand the reasons for your choice of foods for children, but you may need to work out a mutually agreeable compromise in some cases.

Although young infants and mobile infants are fed "on demand" (or at appropriate intervals, adjusted where necessary, to individual needs), feeding may be less individualized for older infants, who can wait a bit longer when hungry. Continue to pay attention to individual needs, but also take group needs into consideration. Older infants eventually can learn to eat as a group on a regular schedule that includes mealtimes and scheduled snacks. However, provision should still be made for the child who is hungry at unscheduled periods or who arrives unfed just after breakfast has been cleared away.

Self-Feeding

Being allowed to touch food is a valuable sensory experience for infants. By handling food and utensils during meals, they develop coordination, the ability to feed themselves, and feelings of competence and autonomy. When child care staff and parents

agree about the value of self-feeding for infants and toddlers, caregivers can feel free to respond to the child's interest in the spoon the first time he or she tries to grab it. Instead of struggling to keep the spoon away from the infant's hand and get it into the mouth, the caregiver can give the infant his or her own spoon with which to explore and experiment while using a second spoon to feed the child. Caregivers can also offer infants and toddlers foods they can pick up with their fingers, removing the food when it appears that the child has had enough to eat rather than allowing it to become only a plaything. In this situation staff and families accept the messiness of self-feeding because they believe that the developmental benefits make it all worthwhile.

Some staff and family members, however, may disapprove of infants feeding themselves, often because of deeply ingrained cultural or family attitudes. For example, in some cultures touching food with fingers is generally prohibited and children are spoon-fed until they can handle utensils with skill. In other cultures it is considered improper or wasteful to do anything with food besides eat it. Some people may feel uncomfortable seeing children's faces and hands smeared with food.

Caregivers who value self-feeding are often concerned that children's development will be affected if they are not allowed to handle food. Early self-feeding is only one of many possible ways, however, to promote exploration and autonomy, and experts point out that the importance of early independence varies from culture to culture. Not everyone agrees that young infants should become independent as quickly as possible. Thus, pro-

Many families have difficulty scheduling regular mealtimes together. Therefore, sociable mealtimes for infants and toddlers in child care are especially important.

grams should handle conflicts about self-feeding, whether among staff members or between staff and families, with sensitivity and respect for the differing perspectives. Any resolution should take into consideration both cultural values and the developmental benefits of self-feeding.

When the disagreement is between program staff and a child's family, family preferences should be taken very seriously while staff may offer information about the developmental value of self-feeding. In the final analysis, caregivers can help children's development the most by working toward harmonious caregiving partnerships, providing as much consistency between child care and home practices as possible, and by nurturing the child's connection with his or her family and culture.

Socializing at Mealtimes

In the past many families shared mealtimes as a daily social occasion. In some homes that custom is still followed, but many families have difficulty scheduling regular mealtimes together. Therefore, sociable mealtimes for infants and toddlers in child care are especially important.

The following general guidelines about social mealtimes apply to children of all age levels:

- Create a calm, pleasant, and unhurried atmosphere so each child has all the time he or she needs to eat.
- Make the environment comfortable, appropriate, and attractive.
- Have small groups of children at each table with an adult.
- Encourage good eating habits and mealtime manners by modeling them.
- Engage children in conversation.
- Provide meals for children when they are hungry.
- Carefully plan to minimize waiting for food.
- Allow children to leave the eating area when they have finished eating and cleaning up.
- Serve a variety of food to offer choices and broaden the children's experiences.
- Avoid using food as punishment or reward.
- Provide opportunities for children to participate in food-related activities and food preparation when they are developmentally ready to do so.

Stop feeding an infant when he or she indicates fullness by turning away or shutting lips, not when the bottle or bowl is empty.

Young and Mobile Infants

A hungry young infant should not have to wait very long to be fed. Infants should not be left crying from hunger but should be fed soon after the crying starts. Stop feeding an infant when he or she indicates fullness by turning away or shutting lips, not when the bottle or bowl is empty.

While young infants are bottle-fed, they should be in the arms of a familiar caregiver in as secluded a place as possible, where they are not distracted by excess noise and activity. The adult should be calm and relaxed, able to focus completely on the child being fed. Whether the adult talks, hums, or sings during the feeding process depends on the individual child and whether the adult's actions enhance the experience.

A little guidance may be needed to teach children to remain at the table while eating.

Mobile infants too young to sit by themselves should be held for bottle or spoon feedings. High chairs are convenient for adults feeding infants but may be unsafe for the mobile, active child who tries to climb in or out. When children are able to sit by themselves and can crawl in and out of a seat, place child-sized seats on the floor around a low table to provide the young, mobile child with safety, autonomy, and a social experience at mealtimes. The children's feet should touch the ground. Small rectangular tables that fit four children comfortably encourage social interaction. The caregiver can easily reach children to provide needed help by sitting at one corner of the table. (See the video *Space to Grow: Creating a Child Care Environment for Infants and Toddlers* for more information about child-sized equipment.)

A little guidance may be needed to teach children to remain at the table while eating. You can provide this guidance by telling them that leaving the table means they have finished and gently trying to get the child to either give up the food or come back to the table with it. As children's understanding of the rule increases, give them a warning, bring them back once, and from then on enforce the rule by not allowing children back to the table once they make the decision to leave.

High chairs were designed for use in the home and are unsuited for child care settings, where they can be a safety hazard. If high chairs are used, make sure they are safe with a wide and stable base and a T-strap. Infants should not be left waiting in high chairs, strapped in while the food is being prepared and other babies are being fed. Nor should children be left in the high chairs when they have finished eating, even though the adult does not consider the mealtime over. A calm, relaxed, attentive, and conversational adult should be part of the feeding process whether the children are sitting on laps, at low tables, or in high chairs.

Older Infants

Older infants usually eat in groups at tables and enjoy helping to set the table and serve themselves. The smaller the group, the less hectic the meal. An adult should be seated with each group. When the adult eats along with the children, he or she is able to model attitudes, manners, and skills, which is the most effective way to teach. By the time children are older infants, the give-and-take interactions of earlier months have become real mealtime conversations about the food, the events of the day, the events to come, news from home, and so on.

Washing Up

The first step in feeding is washing hands—both the caregivers' and the children's. Washing up should be done under running water with soap, not with a wipe or washcloth or in a bowl. (See the handwashing guidelines on page 93.) The last step in the process of feeding infants and toddlers is cleanup. For the young infant who takes only a bottle, the step is very simple and involves rinsing or washing the bottle and nipple. The child often remains clean unless he or she has spit up. A cloth is usually kept close at hand for that purpose.

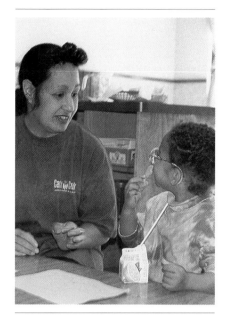

When the adult eats along with the children, he or she is able to model attitudes, manners, and skills, which is the most effective way to teach.

Children who have a hard time with a cup may do better with a straw if they have developed the ability to use a straw.

Mobile infants at the end of a meal may be quite a different story, depending on what they have been eating and whether they have been helping to feed themselves. Use a clean washcloth to wash each child's hands and face, involving the child as much as possible in the washing up process. Bibs will protect clothes, but a change of clothes may be in order now and then after a particularly messy meal.

Older infants can help clean up—both themselves and the table. If an empty dishpan is available, older infants can dispose of their own dirty dishes, wipe up their own place at the table, and go to a low sink and wash their own hands and face with a little help. Of course, some days older infants will be more interested in these activities than on other days, which will determine how much you need to help them with the cleanup.

Infants and Toddlers with Special Needs

Children with special needs may have a special diet. It is important to know whether a child is to have special foods, extra calories, or added or limited intake of certain foods. Parents should be able to provide this information.

Some infants and toddlers need more help with feeding than do others. A child with neurological or motor involvement may not be able drink liquids or swallow solids well. Learn from the parents what the child needs—what has worked at home, what advice they have had about skill building. For example, texture may be an issue. Children who seem to be old enough to chew and swallow table food may need pureed food instead. Some children can improve their eating skills if their mouths are "waked up" with a lip stimulation brush and gum massage. Children who have problems swallowing may need gentle stroking under the chin to help. Children who have a hard time with a cup may do better with a straw if they have developed the ability to use a straw. Careful positioning may help the child feel more secure and therefore able to concentrate on eating instead of being distracted by trying to get comfortable. If the child is able to put feet flat on the floor, that can help. The video *Room at the Table: Meeting Children's Special Needs at Mealtime* offers basic information and some practical suggestions.

Helping the Finicky Eater

Although most children enjoy eating, differences in taste, appetite, and history of eating may make some children very fussy eaters. The following examples show why some children became fussy eaters.

Normal Appetite Decrease

As an infant Myesha had no problem eating. She enjoyed her bottle, and when solids were introduced, she enjoyed them as well. Her mother was used to Myesha's eating everything offered. Then at about the age of two, Myesha's appetite suddenly decreased, and her temper increased. Her mother worried because instead of eating the good-sized meals she used to eat, Myesha started shoving her almost full plate away, saying "s'nuff!"

Myesha's mother did not understand that a dramatic decrease in appetite after the first two years—when the growth rate slows down—is normal. Babies eat so much because they grow so fast; weight gains can be charted on a daily basis for the first months. By two years of age that is no longer the case.

Myesha's mother, used to the infant's large food intake and rapid growth, worried about her child. She tried to get Myesha to eat more. She tried feeding the child, playing games with her, urging her to eat. All the mother did was trigger angry responses. Before long, eating became a big issue, and mother and child were locked in a power struggle.

When Myesha arrived in child care, she brought her eating history with her and immediately established a reputation as a fussy eater. She barely ate anything; although staff did not worry, her mother did—a great deal. Myesha and her food intake were the subject of many parent–caregiver conferences, both formal and informal, until the staff finally convinced the mother to relax and stop making an issue of eating. Myesha is still a light eater but is making normal weight gains, and now no one is worried about her.

Complications of Prematurity

Michael was born prematurely and stayed in the hospital for three months, during which time he encountered a number of life-threatening complications and illnesses. He was fed through a tube directly into his stomach most of those

three months. Learning to suck a nipple while he was coordinating breathing and swallowing was not easy for Michael.

When he came home from the hospital, Michael spent most of his time sleeping and had to be awakened to be fed. He often fell asleep before he had consumed more than an ounce or two. Then he suffered a severe case of diarrhea and became dehydrated, which put him back in the hospital.

Michael's mother was told how important it was that she get a certain amount of food and fluids into Michael and that it was her fault that he was dehydrated. From then on she took a vigorous approach to feeding her son—insisting that he finish his bottles. When he started eating solid foods, she pushed him to eat although he showed little interest.

When Michael entered child care, he was a healthy fifteen-month-old, a little thin but not abnormally so. Although he enjoyed his bottle, he did not like solid foods very much. Michael's mother and the staff together explored ways to improve his enjoyment of solids, discovering what flavors and textures most appealed to him. They found that Michael liked finger food best and they tried to find ways to give him a greater variety of foods he could pick up himself, even though the other babies were eating food that mostly required bowls and spoons.

Unhealthy Eating Habits

Reynaldo, a 24-month-old, recently entered the program. He often refused to eat the food offered at the center, food that consisted of fresh fruit, cooked and raw vegetables, meat, fish, whole-grain bread, and unsweetened cereals. Sometimes Reynaldo would go all day eating almost nothing, and yet he weighed quite a bit more than an average child his age. Concerned about Reynaldo's eating habits and excess weight, the caregiver decided she needed to speak with his mother. The caregiver began the discussion by telling Reynaldo's mother that he ate very little at the center. The caregiver then asked if she had any insights about why this was happening. Reynaldo's mother explained that Reynaldo's grandmother, who lived with the family, liked to give Reynaldo doughnuts, chips, cola, and candy. Reynaldo had learned to like those foods.

The mother said that she was also concerned but didn't know what to do. Together the caregiver and the mother formed a plan to continue offering Reynaldo the natural, wholesome food served at the center and to cut down on the junk food available at home. When he could no longer consume junk food at home in the evening, Reynaldo's daytime appetite increased, and he began to eat selectively the food served at the center. He still does not eat the balanced diet the staff would prefer, but both his eating habits and his weight have improved.

General Guidelines

Although each finicky eater has a separate story and needs to be considered individually, there are some general approaches to adopt:

- Find out more about the child's eating habits at home.
- Work closely with the parent both to understand the behavior and to look for different mealtime strategies for the child.
- If you have concerns about a child's growth, discuss them with the parents and recommend an evaluation by the child's health care provider. If the child is gaining weight normally, do not worry about the amount consumed.
- Offer only nourishing food in attractive and *small* servings.
- Stay out of power struggles. One way to do that is to give the child some choices.
- Take as much of the negative emotional tone out of mealtimes as possible.

- See whether altering the environment in which the food is presented makes a difference. For example, does the child eat better when the meal is a "picnic" outside? Does the child eat better without other children around?

Information about feeding needs to pass freely between caregiver and parent on a regular basis. The knowledge makes a difference to the caregiver if an infant arrives without having eaten. How else is the caregiver to know, when the baby cries, whether the cry is from hunger or for some other reason? At the end of the day, the parent of an older infant needs to know when the child last ate and how much, in order to plan dinner.

The information can be exchanged informally when parents and primary caregivers see each other regularly at the beginning and end of the day. However, changing shifts may get in the way of that informal communication system, in which case a written system is called for. Some centers have chalkboards to record the information daily. Others have forms to fill out for each child. Still others keep the information in notebooks available to parents. However the recordkeeping is done, the flow of information is vital to the caregiver's and the parent's job as well as to each child's well-being. Programs receiving funds from the Child Care Food Program must comply with its reporting and recordkeeping requirements.

Points to Consider

1. How well do your feeding routines reflect your program's philosophy? Look for examples of the ways in which you carry out your goals through your approaches to feeding. Consider goals of health and safety as well as of physical, social, emotional, and cognitive development. Is increasing independence one of your goals? Do your feeding routines promote that goal?

2. What ways have you found to balance the feeding needs of infants and toddlers with your own convenience and comfort?

3. How consistent are the feeding routines in your program? Are the routines full of daily surprises for the children, or can the children learn to predict what will happen and thus add to their sense of security?

4. How well do your feeding routines for each child match those of his or her home? Do you have continual communication with parents in order to provide as much consistency as possible between home and day care?

5. Does each child get individual attention during feeding routines? Are the routines set up in such a way that you have the opportunity for one-on-one interactions?

Suggested Resources

Books and Articles

American Academy of Pediatrics, Committee on Infectious Diseases. *2000 Red Book Report of the Committee on Infectious Diseases* (24th edition). Elk Grove Village, Ill.: American Academy of Pediatrics, 2000.

The first new edition in three years advances the *Red Book*'s mission for the twenty-first century with the most current information on clinical manifestations, etiology, epidemiology, diagnosis, and treatment of more than 200 childhood infectious diseases. It was developed with the assistance and advice of hundreds of physician contributors from across the country. The new edition contains many significant revisions, updates, and additions to its authoritative content.

Berman, Christine. *Meals Without Squeals.* Palo Alto, Calif.: Bull Publishing Co., 1997.

This book offers information on children's growth accompanied by age-specific, child-tested recipes. The author explains ways to solve common feeding problems and offer children positive experiences with food.

Berman, Christine. *Teaching Children About Food,* Palo Alto, Calif.: Bull Publishing, 1991.

Written as a companion book to *Meals Without Squeals,* this book offers parents and professionals cooking and gardening activities for children, tips to help children become smart consumers, ideas for supporting cultural diversity in food choices and preparation, and ways to convey an understanding of the relationship between food and our environment.

Brazelton, T. Berry. *Infants and Mothers: Differences in Development.* New York: Delacorte Press, 1983.

Describes how temperamental differences influence the lives and care of infants.

Gerber, Magda. "Caring for Infants with Respect: The RIE Approach," *Zero to Three* (February 1984), 1–3.

Presents Magda Gerber's approach to caring for infants and toddlers: she recommends that caregivers always respect babies.

Gerber, Magda, and Allan Johnson. *Your Self-Confident Baby: How to Encourage Your Child's Natural Abilities from the Very Start.* New York: John Wiley & Sons, 1998.

Presents Gerber's philosophy of respect for the autonomy and competence of infants and toddlers in relation to all aspects of care, including feeding, diapering, and napping.

Gonzalez-Mena, Janet. *Multicultural Issues in Child Care* (Third edition). Mountain View, Calif.: Mayfield Publishing Co., 2001.

The chapter on feeding explores cultural differences in beliefs, values, attitudes, approaches, and practices.

Gonzalez-Mena, Janet. *Tips and Tidbits: A Book for Family Child Care Providers.* Washington, D.C.: National Association for the Education of Young Children, 1991.

Offers ideas for handling eating or napping difficulties, squabbling, "potty mouth," and other day-to-day matters that arise in a child care provider's life.

Gonzalez-Mena, Janet, and Dianne W. Eyer. *Infants, Toddlers, and Caregivers* (Fifth edition). Mountain View, Calif.: Mayfield Publishing Co., 2001.

Discusses feeding infants and toddlers as part of the caregiving routines that make up a major part of the child care curriculum.

Healthy Young Children: A Manual for Programs. Edited by A. S. Kendrick, R. Kaufman, and K. P. Messenger. Washington, D.C.: National Association for the Education of Young Children, 1995.

This basic manual is used in early childhood programs to promote the health and safety of children, staff, and families. Designed for ease in finding information, it is frequently used as a textbook.

Keeping Kids Healthy: Preventing and Managing Communicable Disease in Child Care. Sacramento: California Department of Education, 1995.

This manual is designed for use in child care settings with children from birth to five years. It contains chapters on understanding, preventing, recognizing, and managing communicable disease. A list of resources is included.

Looking In, Looking Out: Redefining Child Care and Early Education in a Diverse Society. San Francisco: California Tomorrow, 1996.

Offers new research and insights into examining the role of diversity in all aspects of care.

A Manual for Parents and Professionals. Edited by Magda Gerber. Los Angeles: Resources for Infant Educarers, 1978.

Explains how the RIE method works and gives practical advice about how to put respect into caregiving routines, such as feeding. Available from Resources for Infant Educarers (RIE), 1550 Murray Circle, Los Angeles, CA 90026.

Nash, M., and C. Tate. "Nutrition and Feeding," in *Better Baby Care: A Book for Family Day Care Providers.* Washington, D.C.: The Children's Foundation, 1986, pp. 79–84.

Provides information about how to feed infants and toddlers. Although written for family child care providers, the information will be useful to center caregivers as well.

Phillips, Carol Brunson, and Renatta Cooper. "Cultural Dimensions of Feeding Relationships," *Zero to Three* (June 1992), 10–13.

Explores cultural differences as they relate to feeding.

Samuels, Mike, and Nancy Samuels. *The Well Baby Book.* New York: Summit Books, 1979.

Examines babies' needs and health issues from a holistic health perspective.

Satter, Ellyn. *Child of Mine: How to Get Your Child to Eat, But Not Too Much.* Palo Alto, Calif.: Bull Publishing, 1987.

This book addresses concerns about snacking, refusal to eat vegetables, and many other issues that arise in the relationship between parents, children, and food. Presents strategies and support in an easy-to-read format.

Satter, Ellyn. *Child of Mine: Feeding with Love and Good Sense.* Palo Alto, Calif.: Bull Publishing, 1991.

This book for parents and professionals provides information about basic nutrition for infants and young children and ways to feed them so that autonomy and trust are developed. Other topics include breast-feeding, bottle-feeding, learning to eat "grownups'" food, and normal growth from infancy through preschool.

Setting Up for Infant/Toddler Care: Guidelines for Centers and Family Child Care Homes (Revised edition). Edited by Annabelle Godwin and Lorraine Schrag. Washington, D.C.: National Association for the Education of Young Children, 1996.

Includes practical information regarding business aspects of setting up a child care program. Experts describe how to promote all areas of a child's development.

Spock, Benjamin M., and Michael Rothenberg. *Dr. Spock's Baby and Child Care: Fortieth Anniversary Edition.* New York: E. P. Dutton, 1985.

An update of Dr. Spock's classic, the book has useful advice on the care of infants and toddlers.

Thoman, Evelyn B., and Sue Browder. *Born Dancing: The Relaxed Parents' Guide to Making Babies Smart with Love.* New York: Harper and Row, 1987.

Explores how babies communicate and describes how caregivers can trust, respect, and understand babies' unspoken language and natural rhythms, thus engaging in a dance with the infants.

Audiovisuals

Caring for Our Children. Elk Grove Village, Ill.: American Academy of Pediatrics, 1995. Six 30-minute videocassettes.

The six videos show how to comply with the health and safety guidelines set forth in the manual of the same title. Each video clearly presents the appropriate steps to take to ensure safe and healthy out-of-home care.

Day Care: A Comprehensive Look—Infants and Toddlers (Part I). Tuckahoe, N.Y.: Campus Films Distributors Corp., 1979. Filmstrip, color, 90 slides; sound on cassette; printed guide.

Discusses the importance of attending to the total development of the child. Emphasizes the importance of daily routines as a time for children to learn and acquire good feelings about the world. Approximately ten slides show how feeding can be enjoyable for both child and caregiver. Available from Campus Films Distributors Corp., 24 Depot Sq., Tuckahoe, NY 10707.

Early Childhood Training Series: Contrasting Perspectives. Barrington, Ill.: Magna Systems, 1996. Videocassette, color, 27 minutes. Workbook with discussion questions.

Designed to show contrasts and spark dialogue, this video depicts variations on themes of independence, interdependence, and individuality in day-to-day caregiving. Among the questions addressed: Are there right and wrong ways when it comes to sleeping, eating, playing, and learning?

Early Childhood Training Series: Diversity, Independence, and Individuality. Barrington, Ill.: Magna Systems, 1996. Videocassette, color, 27 minutes. Workbook with discussion questions.

Focuses on diverse reactions to scenes of children learning to be independent individuals. This video shows how valuing independence and individuality defines teaching approaches and feeding, toileting, and napping practices.

Feeding Skills: Your Baby's Early Years. Los Angeles: Churchill Films, 1981. Videocassette and film, color, 24 1/2 minutes.

Gives information on helping children from age two weeks to two years to acquire eating skills; discusses the importance of feeding times to the baby's development of trust. Includes information on nutrition and food preparation. Available from SVE & Churchill Media, 6677 No. Northwest Hwy., Chicago, IL 60631. Telephone: (800) 829-1900.

Flexible, Fearful, or Feisty: The Different Temperaments of Infants and Toddlers. Sacramento: California Department of Education (with WestEd), 1990. Videocassette, color, 29 minutes; printed guide.

Identifies nine temperamental traits exhibited by infants and toddlers that are typically grouped into three temperamental types, described in the video as flexible, fearful, and feisty. Provides caregivers with techniques for dealing with the differences between individual infants and toddlers in group child care settings.

Getting in Tune: Creating Nurturing Relationships with Infants and Toddlers. Sacramento: California Department of Education (with WestEd), 1988. Videocassette, color, 24 minutes; printed guide.

Presents the responsive process, which includes three steps: watching, asking, and adapting. Helps the caregiver learn what a young child needs and how best to respond to that need.

Ingredients for a Good Start. Sacramento: California Department of Education (with WestEd), 1994. Videocassette, color, 25 minutes; printed guide.

Relates mealtimes to development and gives information about how to provide healthy foods that include the food pyramid for infants, toddlers, and preschoolers and how to develop healthy habits.

It's Not Just Routine: Feeding, Diapering, and Napping Infants and Toddlers (Second edition). Sacramento: California Department of Education (with WestEd), 2000. Videocassette, color, 24 minutes; printed guide.

Updated version demonstrates how to carry out feeding, diapering, and napping routines with infants and toddlers. Describes important elements of the setting and health issues, including proper hand washing and nutrition. Emphasizes the quality of the experience for the child and the caregiver.

Room at the Table: Meeting Children's Special Needs at Mealtime. Sacramento: California Department of Education (with WestEd), 1996. Videocassette, color, 23 minutes; printed guide.

All children are capable of growing, learning, and responding to love no matter what their abilities as long as they have caring adults who believe in them. This video has valuable information on ways to include children with special needs in child care programs and to adapt mealtime to those needs. The second half shows caregivers and experts demonstrating exciting techniques for meeting children's needs.

Space to Grow: Creating a Child Care Environment for Infants and Toddlers. Sacramento: California Department of Education (with WestEd), 1988. Videocassette, color, 22 minutes; printed guide.

Presents concepts to consider in setting up feeding and eating areas for infants.

Information Hotline

California Child Care Health Line: 1-800-333-3212

This hotline provides child care health and safety information Monday through Thursday, 8 a.m. to 4 p.m.

Section Three:
Diapering and Toileting

When an adult has more than one infant or toddler to care for, the adult's attention must be divided. Some children tend to draw more attention than others because of their charm, others because of their difficult behavior, still others because of their ability to engage adults directly. In every group of infants and toddlers, there are some children who do not command as much attention as others. They may be easygoing or cautious in temperament, or they may simply attract less attention than other children. All babies in child care, whether they demand it or not, need regular, focused attention from an adult—preferably the same adult each time. Diapering is a built-in opportunity to give that attention.

Diapering—A Social and Learning Activity

Perhaps the least favorite of the caregiving routines for many adults (though not necessarily for children), diapering nevertheless offers many opportunities for focused, one-to-one interactions.

The child being diapered must have the caregiver's focused attention.

When used to the fullest, those many diaper changes enhance social development and all kinds of learning. Diapering can become a valuable activity instead of a chore.

Diapering becomes a constructive experience for the child when three principles are followed:

1. The attention of the caregiver is focused on the child and the task at hand.
2. The caregiver treats the child with respect.
3. Talking with the child is part of the experience.

Focused Attention

When a caregiver is entirely responsible or shares responsibility for several children, it is often difficult to give only one child focused attention—yet that is what must happen during diapering. Everyone on the caregiving team needs to agree that focused attention is important. Caregivers support each other by covering for the caregiver who is diapering. In programs where this system works, one caregiver can focus on the baby being diapered and remain assured that the group is in good hands. Still, the caregiver remains aware of the rest of the group in case the other caregivers should need additional help with a sudden problem.

When a caregiver is alone with several babies, as is usually the case in family child care, giving focused attention is more difficult. The caregiver can still give close attention to the baby being diapered if the environment has been set up to be entirely safe for every child in it. Babies can play on their own while the caregiver's attention is on diapering. Of course, the caregiver in these circumstances will still keep an eye out for what is going on elsewhere—even if only from the corner of an eye. Experienced caregivers get to be very good at giving that kind of dual attention. They can focus directly on one child while they are still aware of the several other children in their charge.

Respectful Diapering

In a respectful diapering sequence, the caregiver approaches the baby slowly, making sure that he or she is in the baby's line of vision and that the baby is not surprised at the approach. The caregiver takes time to see where the baby's attention is focused. If the baby is involved with a toy or with another baby, the caregiver does not interrupt right away. Instead the baby is given time to become used to the caregiver's presence. After the baby has had enough time to take notice of the caregiver, the care-

Diapering with respect includes attending to the whole infant or toddler.

giver announces that he or she is going to change the baby's diaper and gives the child time to respond. Holding out his or her arms, the caregiver then announces that he or she is going to pick up the baby—and again allows time for a response. When the baby seems to understand what is to happen (depending on the age), the caregiver picks up and carries the infant to the diaper-changing station.

The procedure may be drawn out into a lengthy transition or it may happen quite rapidly. The point is to get the baby to focus on what will happen without feeling interrupted or distracted. The video *Respectfully Yours: Magda Gerber's Approach to Professional Infant/Toddler Care* further explains the concept of respect.

At the changing table, the caregiver continues to announce what will happen before it does, giving the baby a chance to take in the information. ("First, I'm going to undo your overalls.") The caregiver asks for the baby's cooperation, whenever possible, involving the infant in the process. ("Please lift up your bottom for me.") The caregiver helps the child focus both on the process itself and on the child's own body and its sensations. ("That's wet, isn't it? But the water's nice and warm—feel how warm it is.")

The conversation centers on what is happening then and there. If the baby wants to play—blowing bubbles at the caregiver, for example—the caregiver responds, joining in the game and pausing in the diapering process. Then, when appropriate, the caregiver brings the baby's attention back to the task at hand.

If you think of doing something with the baby rather than doing something to the baby, you will see the difference between a respectful diapering and one that is not. The message to the child from respectful diapering is: "I care about you; nothing about you disgusts me. This is a task we must work on together to get done; we can both enjoy it while we are doing it. You can learn something about yourself, the world, and me by paying attention to what is happening, and I will help you pay attention."

Object-Oriented Diapering

In contrast to the respectful way of diapering is the object-oriented way. In this procedure, the infant is snatched up in the middle of whatever he or she is doing and plopped on the diaper-changing station with no explanation. The infant is handed a toy to play with. From then on the infant's upper half is ignored

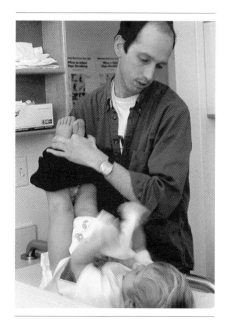

If you think of doing something with the baby rather than doing something to the baby, you will see the difference between a respectful diapering and one that is not.

You should never have to leave the diapering area during a diapering.

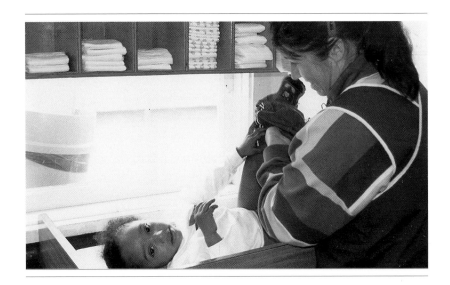

while the bottom half gets cursory attention from a caregiver who, with a frown and a wrinkled nose, cleans the child while carrying on a conversation with someone else. The child gets a very different message from that kind of diapering.

The irony is that the object-oriented way is not necessarily faster and more efficient than the respectful way, even with all the waiting that may be required by being respectful. An experienced caregiver knows that only at certain stages do babies take diapering lying down. As soon as babies can turn over, they realize they have a choice in the matter, and they may spend as much energy trying to get off the changing table as the caregiver does keeping them on and getting them changed. So if the caregiver is working for fast, efficient diapering, he or she is better off being respectful and trying for cooperation rather than dealing in other, less respectful ways that can easily lead to a struggle with the child.

The Older Infant's Diapering

By the end of the mobile infant stage, most infants go back to their earlier, more willing selves. As infants get older, they can be truly helpful, holding still when necessary, putting feet into pant legs, raising bottoms, and holding them up while the caregiver slides the diaper underneath. By that age the infants who have been involved in the diapering process as active participants can be distinguished from those who have been treated as passive recipients of a service performed on them.

Of course, a diapering process that does not take the individual caregiver's style into consideration is not worth much.

However, once caregivers incorporate the spirit of respect into their systems, carrying out respectful diaperings in individual styles is not difficult.

A Convenient Environment

Adult convenience is another important consideration in the diapering process. The secret to success is in arranging the environment. All diapering supplies should be at hand. The diapering area should be near a source of warm water. Provisions for disposing of used diapers should be within reach. You should never have to leave the diapering area during a diapering. (If you do, take the baby with you—never leave a baby unattended on a diaper-changing station.)

Convenience requires preparation and organization. Nothing is worse than reaching for a diaper and finding the cupboard empty or wanting a clean pair of overalls and discovering they are in the diaper bag in the child's cubby. Planning ahead is vital to a smooth diapering process. The videos *Space to Grow: Creating a Child Care Environment for Infants and Toddlers* and *It's Not Just Routine* (Second edition) show convenient diapering arrangements.

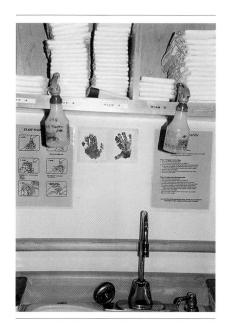

Sanitation Procedures

Sanitation is essential. The diaper-changing station must be an elevated surface used only for diapering and away from food preparation or serving areas. It should not be a kitchen counter, eating table, couch, bed, or the floor. Sanitation procedures must be followed carefully. You should develop procedures that satisfy licensing and health requirements and post them in every diapering area. A sample set of procedures follows:

1. Check to be sure the diaper area has been sanitized since the last diapering. If not, discard used paper, spray with a bleach solution, and put clean paper down.
2. Remove the used diaper and dispose of it in a covered container.
3. Wipe the child with a clean, moist cloth or baby wipe. Wipe girls from front to back to prevent urinary and vaginal infections. Dispose of the used cloth or the wipe in the container provided. If gloves are used, remove and discard them. *Gloves must be removed after the dirty part and before the clean part of the diapering to prevent the spread of germs.*

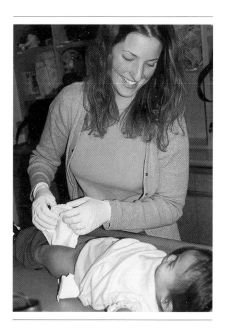

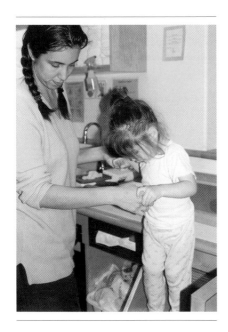

4. Put a clean diaper and clean clothes on the child.

5. Wash the child's hands under running water. Babies often touch their bottoms and the diaper-changing station, which are loaded with germs. Washing their hands after diapering helps prevent the spread of germs from the diapering procedure, and it begins to teach them the lifelong hygiene habit of washing hands after going to the bathroom. Return the child to the play area.

6. Clean and sanitize the diapering area: discard used paper in the container provided, spray with a bleach solution, wipe lightly with a paper towel to spread the bleach solution around, and discard the paper towel. Put down a clean paper when the bleach disinfectant has air dried.

7. Wash hands thoroughly.

Gloves are not necessary for every diapering. However, the use of disposable latex gloves is advised, even if not required, whenever the caregiver has open cuts, scratches, or sores; if the child has diarrhea; or if there is blood in the stool. If gloves are used, remember to remove and discard them after wiping the child's bottom and before putting on the clean diaper and clothes. (See the video *It's Not Just Routine* [Second edition] for a demonstration of the proper use of gloves.)

Toileting—Readiness in Three Developmental Areas

Toilet training or learning starts in infancy when babies are treated as partners in their diaper changes. As infants become older, they become more and more aware of their bodily functions and eventually begin to learn to control them. Toilet learning is a natural process that occurs over a long period of time. Using the toilet regularly occurs when the child achieves readiness in three areas: physical, cognitive, and emotional.

Physical Readiness

A clue to approaching physical readiness is when an older infant announces after urinating or defecating, "Me go peepee (poopoo)!" It is important for the caregiver to respond positively to such an announcement. It is also important for the caregiver to know what words the child uses for bodily functions in order to understand such a noteworthy announcement. Find out from the parents when they enroll their child—do not take a chance on misunderstanding.

A further clue to approaching readiness is when the child stays dry for several hours at a time. That means the bladder can hold more and for longer, a necessary prerequisite of success in using the toilet. Holding on is an important physical step. Letting go is another one. Success in using the toilet means that the child not only must hold on until he or she is bare-bottomed and actually on the toilet but also must be able to relax the sphincter muscles that close the bladder or rectum.

That kind of fine-tuned control takes much longer in some children than in others. Using the toilet is a more complicated process than it seems to those of us who learned it long ago and do not even think about it. For the beginner, the process is a different matter entirely.

Another sign of physical readiness is when the child can handle his or her own clothing, as long as the process does not involve complicated unbuttoning or untying. When signs of physical readiness appear, children should be dressed in simple clothes rather than the cute little overalls and one-piece jumpsuits that work so well with younger infants. Pants with elastic waistbands are easiest for toddlers to handle—both boys and girls. Of course, a parent who has just invested in a whole wardrobe of colorful size two overalls may not want to hear from the caregiver about the need for a change of style. Be respectful with parents who have different ideas about how the child should be dressed.

Cognitive Readiness

Physical readiness is not enough—cognitive readiness is also necessary. The child must both be capable of using the toilet and understand what it is that he or she is expected to do. Being in child care facilitates this understanding as children see other children learning to use the toilet and model themselves after older classmates. Such an opportunity is an added advantage of multiage settings.

Emotional Readiness

Most important of all is emotional readiness. If a child understands and is capable but is not *willing,* the child is not completely ready. Delays in emotional readiness sometimes occur because toilet training is emphasized over toilet learning. The child may be pushed too soon or too hard, leading to a power struggle over using the toilet. If that is the case, the best approach is to lay off for a while and continue to strive for a partnership in the toileting process. Eventually most children will stop being negative about using the toilet. Of course, the power struggle is

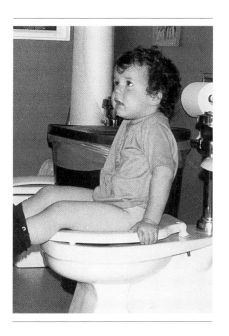

The needed control for using the toilet comes later to some children than others.

more likely to be between the child and parent, and the caregiver may not have much control over what is happening there. Conferring with the parent(s) is essential.

Parental Viewpoints

It is important that the caregiver discusses toilet learning with the parent(s) before any difficult situations arise. The caregiver needs to find out the parents' ideas, perceptions, and goals for their child in this area of development and explain his or her philosophy. When viewpoints differ, the caregiver should try to see the issue from the parents' perspective.

Often a problem occurs when the parents and the caregiver have different definitions of toilet learning. The following definition is the one accepted by most caregivers: Toilet learning is the process by which a child learns to take responsibility for his or her own elimination. Toilet learning is complete when the child can get to the toilet independently; take off his or her own clothes enough to use and flush the toilet; wipe himself or herself; and wash his or her hands afterwards.

Some parents see toilet learning very differently. They see it as something for which the adult has primary responsibility. Readiness is not a concern. The goal is dry clothes rather than the child's independence. Parents with this view sometimes start getting their child to use the toilet at the end of the first year of life or earlier. Some parents are successful in "catching" their child and putting him or her on the toilet and therefore are able to minimize or eliminate the need for diapers. This method is common practice in many parts of the world and is not that unusual in this country.

Most parents who define toilet training in such a way probably do not ask caregivers to take the responsibility for "catching" their child because of the number of children in the program. Parents may, however, have difficulty understanding or accepting the caregiver's reluctance to assist the child with toileting as early as the parent believes appropriate. It is important to work through conflicts such as these and reach some sort of understanding that satisfies both the parent and the caregiver and also considers the child's and the program's needs.

Emotional Issues

Feelings are an important consideration in any discussion of toilet learning. Bodily functions in general, and toileting specifically, call forth a variety of feelings in adults. Many adults had

Parents and caregivers may have different definitions of toilet training.

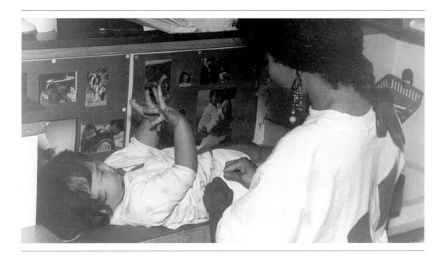

harsh toilet training experiences as children or were taught that bodily functions are "dirty" and "shameful." Anyone who is going into infant or toddler care needs to become aware of his or her attitude toward such fundamental issues and come to grips with and resolve the leftover feelings that can be passed on to children.

It is vital to healthy emotional development that children learn to accept their bodies, the functions of those bodies, and the products of those functions as natural, wholesome parts of themselves. Children can do that only if the adults around them are positive or at least matter-of-fact about changing and training them. The words adults use reflect their attitudes. Avoid words like *stinky, filthy,* or *disgusting* at the diaper-changing station or in the bathroom. Children must be taught sanitary procedures, but this can be done without using words that have negative connotations. (There is more on this subject in Section Six, "Preparing, Ordering, and Maintaining the Environment.")

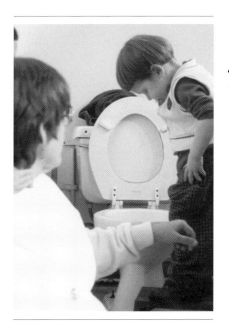

Make toilet learning a pleasant experience. Do not push the child. Be matter-of-fact about accidents. Do not scold or punish. The less emotion involved, the more likely you will stay out of a power struggle that you cannot win. After all, elimination is one process you cannot control in another person, and it is one in which children can take the upper hand if they feel a need to.

To help older infants with toilet learning, low child-sized toilets are far preferable to child-sized seats on adult toilets or potty chairs. Children have to be lifted on and off the higher seats and may feel very insecure while up there. That insecurity may inhibit their muscle control and work against the toilet learning. Potty chairs are not recommended for child care because they are more difficult to sanitize properly.

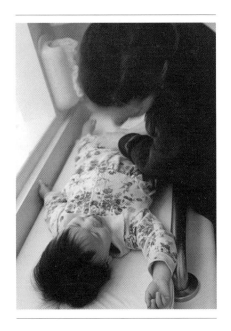

Pay attention to the child's accomplishments but do not get overly emotional about them. For example, briefly praise beginners for telling you after they have had a bowel movement in their diapers. Mention how pleased you are when a child has been dry for several hours. And, of course, show your enthusiasm when the child eliminates in the toilet for the first time.

Work with parents to determine when the child is ready for toilet learning, and let the child's readiness be your guide. Consulting with the parents about the child's readiness ensures their cooperation. Consistency between home and the child care program will make the child's learning more effective.

Recording the Information

As is true with feeding, the more communication between parent(s) and caregiver about diapering and toileting, the better. Information should be exchanged about the consistency and frequency of stools and, for the very young breast-fed baby, the frequency of urination (how wet the diapers are indicates how much breast milk the baby is getting). The more both the caregiver and the parent know what to expect, the more easily they can meet the individual child's needs.

A simple chart by the diaper-changing station or bathroom will do to record information concerning the time of changes, the time of bowel movement(s), and anything unusual about the stool. For the older infant in training, the chart can be simpler, merely noting the number of times the child went to the bathroom and when the child moved his or her bowels.

The information should be available to the parent at pickup time. It may be included with the feeding record or be posted at the diapering area, with a note for the parents near the sign-out sheet if something unusual needs to be brought to their attention. For children in training, it is important to know the last time they went to the bathroom and whether they need some reminding or direction.

When children are cared for by more than one adult, records become important daily sources of information. Without them a child might become constipated because the caregiver thought the child was moving his or her bowels at home and the parent(s) thought the child was doing it in child care. Or a child who is just learning to use the toilet might have an accident on the way home because no one realized that several hours had elapsed since the child had gone to the toilet.

Points to Consider

1. Are you aware of the emotional climate around diapering and toilet training? How can you promote a positive atmosphere?

2. Do you use diapering times as opportunities for one-to-one interactions? Are both adult and child fully attentive to the experience?

3. How well does your diapering and toilet learning routine fit into the overall program structure and philosophy?

4. How can good communication between parent(s) and caregiver help the child receive consistency in diapering and toilet learning?

5. What ideas do you have for resolving the conflicts that may arise when parent(s) and caregiver disagree on the timing or procedures of diapering or toilet learning?

Suggested Resources

Books and Articles

American Academy of Pediatrics, Committee on Infectious Diseases. *2000 Red Book Report of the Committee on Infectious Diseases* (24th edition). Elk Grove Village, Ill.: American Academy of Pediatrics, 2000.

The first new edition in three years advances the *Red Book*'s mission for the twenty-first century with the most current information on clinical manifestations, etiology, epidemiology, diagnosis, and treatment of more than 200 childhood infectious diseases. It was developed with the

The more communications between parent(s) and caregiver about diapering and toileting, the better.

assistance and advice of hundreds of physician contributors from across the country. The new edition contains many significant revisions, updates, and additions to its authoritative content.

Cole, Joanna. *Parents' Book of Toilet Training.* New York: Ballantine Books, 1988.

Emphasizes waiting until a child is physically, cognitively, and emotionally ready for toilet training.

Gerber, Magda. "Caring for Infants with Respect: The RIE Approach," *Zero to Three* (February 1984), 1–3.

Presents Magda Gerber's approach to caring for infants and toddlers: she recommends that caregivers always respect babies.

Gerber, Magda, and Allan Johnson. *Your Self-Confident Baby: How to Encourage Your Child's Natural Abilities from the Very Start.* New York: John Wiley & Sons, 1998.

Presents Gerber's philosophy of respect for the autonomy and competence of infants and toddlers in relation to all aspects of care, including feeding, diapering, and napping.

Gonzalez-Mena, Janet. *Multicultural Issues in Child Care* (Third edition). Mountain View, Calif.: Mayfield Publishing Co., 2001.

Discusses diverse views of diapering and toilet training and explores cultural differences in beliefs, values, attitudes, approaches, and practices.

Gonzalez-Mena, Janet, and Dianne W. Eyer. *Infants, Toddlers, and Caregivers* (Fifth edition). Mountain View, Calif.: Mayfield Publishing Co., 2001.

Discusses diapering infants and toddlers and toilet training as a part of the caregiving routines that make up a major part of the child care curriculum.

Healthy Young Children: A Manual for Programs. Edited by A. S. Kendrick, R. Kaufman, and K. P. Messenger. Washington, D.C.: National Association for the Education of Young Children, 1995.

This basic manual is used in early childhood programs to promote the health and safety of children, staff, and families. Designed for ease in finding information, it is frequently used as a textbook.

Keeping Kids Healthy: Preventing and Managing Communicable Disease in Child Care. Sacramento: California Department of Education, 1995.

This manual is designed for use in child care settings with children from birth to five years. It contains chapters on understanding, preventing, recognizing, and managing communicable disease. A list of resources is included.

Leavitt, Robin L., and Brenda K. Eheart. "Managing Routines Within the Daily Schedule," in *Toddler Day Care: A Guide to Responsive Caregiving.* Lexington, Mass.: Lexington Books, 1985, pp. 52–54.

Covers basic sanitation procedures as well as steps to take to diaper a child in a respectful way.

A Manual for Parents and Professionals. Edited by Magda Gerber. Los Angeles: Resources for Infant Educarers, 1978.

Explains how the RIE method works and gives practical advice about how to put respect into caregiving routines such as diapering. Available from Resources for Infant Educarers (RIE), 1550 Murray Circle, Los Angeles, CA 90026.

Samuels, Mike, and Nancy Samuels. *The Well Baby Book.* New York: Summit Books, 1979.

Examines babies' needs and health issues from a holistic health perspective.

Setting Up for Infant/Toddler Care: Guidelines for Centers and Family Child Care Homes (Revised edition). Edited by Annabelle Godwin and Lorraine Schrag. Washington, D.C.: National Association for the Education of Young Children, 1996.

Includes practical information regarding business aspects of setting up a child care program. Experts describe how to promote all areas of a child's development.

Thoman, Evelyn B., and Sue Browder. *Born Dancing: The Relaxed Parents' Guide to Making Babies Smart with Love.* New York: Harper and Row, 1987.

Explores how babies communicate and describes how caregivers can trust, respect, and understand babies' unspoken language and natural rhythms, thus engaging in a dance with the infants.

Audiovisuals

Caring for Our Children. Elk Grove Village, Ill.: American Academy of Pediatrics, 1995. Six 30-minute videocassettes.

The six videos show how to comply with the health and safety guidelines set forth in the manual bearing the same title. Each video clearly presents the appropriate steps to take to ensure safe and healthy out-of-home care.

The Developing Child: Toddlerhood. Barrington, Ill.: Magna Systems, 1992. Two videocassettes, color, 27 minutes each.

Explores issues in autonomy and independence: eating, toileting, and sleeping.

Diversity and Communication. Early Childhood Training Series. Barrington, Ill.: Magna Systems, 1992. Videocassette, color, 27 minutes; workbook with discussion guide.

Highlights communication blocks between parents and caregivers and points out ways of creating connections using sample areas of disagreement, including toilet training.

Flexible, Fearful, or Feisty: The Different Temperaments of Infants and Toddlers. Sacramento: California Department of Education (with WestEd), 1990. Videocassette, color, 29 minutes; printed guide.

Identifies nine temperamental traits exhibited by infants and toddlers that are typically grouped into three temperamental types, described in the video as flexible, fearful, and feisty. Provides caregivers with techniques for dealing with the differences between individual infants and toddlers in group child care settings.

Getting in Tune: Creating Nurturing Relationships with Infants and Toddlers. Sacramento: California Department of Education (with WestEd), 1988. Videocassette, color, 24 minutes; printed guide.

Presents the "responsive process," which includes three steps: watching, asking, and adapting. Helps the caregiver learn what a young child needs and how best to respond to that need.

It's Not Just Routine: Feeding, Diapering, and Napping Infants and Toddlers (Second edition). Sacramento: California

Department of Education (with WestEd), 2000. Videocassette, color, 24 minutes; printed guide.

Updated version of the video demonstrates proper hand-washing; discusses the use of gloves (not recommended for routine diapering) and other tips for safe, healthy diapering. Attention is given to the setting, safety and health issues, and the quality of the experience for the child and the caregiver.

Respectfully Yours: Magda Gerber's Approach to Professional Infant/Toddler Care. Sacramento: California Department of Education (with WestEd), 1988. Videocassette, color, 55 minutes; printed guide.

Presents Magda Gerber's philosophy based on respecting the baby.

Space to Grow: Creating a Child Care Environment for Infants and Toddlers. Sacramento: California Department of Education (with WestEd), 1988. Videocassette, color, 22 minutes; printed guide.

Presents eight environmental issues that need to be considered when arranging an environment for infants and toddlers.

Information Hotline

California Child Care Health Line: 1-800-333-3212
This hotline provides child care health and safety information Monday through Thursday, 8 a.m. to 4 p.m.

Section Four:
Dressing and Bathing

Dressing and bathing are examples of those one-to-one experiences that are so vital to good child care. These routines can be a source of pleasure for the caregiver and the child if the child is encouraged to become involved in the process. Dressing and bathing are also good opportunities for the child to learn body parts because the body can be discussed naturally during both routines.

Dressing and Undressing

Dressing and undressing allow time not only to change the child's clothes but to respond to the child as well. With the young infant, pay attention to babbles and coos and enjoy and return smiles. If the mobile infant starts a peek-a-boo game, pick up on it. With older infants, be responsive to games they may initiate; for instance, which arm or leg to dress first or which piece of clothing to put on first. These types of responses come

Dressing and bathing are examples of those one-to-one experiences that are so vital to good child care.

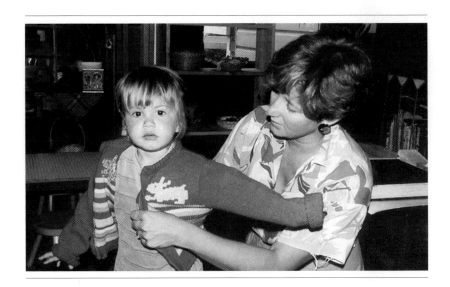

naturally to most adults but are mentioned here because when you are responsible for several children and the day gets hectic, you may rush through tasks such as dressing instead of relaxing and doing what comes naturally and takes extra time.

Young Infants

Dressing young infants may seem a little like dressing dolls. Their thumbs stick out at odd angles and catch in sleeves. Their elbows and knees do not bend precisely when you need them to. You need to handle infants and talk to them as human beings, not as lifeless objects. The respect you give early on pays off later as infants gain control of their thumbs and knees. They become cooperative partners before you realize they have, and the hand you struggled so hard with last month slides easily into the sleeve on its own accord this month.

Many young infants dislike being bare and may cry during the changing process. Even though they may be unhappy and you are anxious to get the task over with, it is still important to be respectful. Tell them what you are going to do before you do it: "I'm going to pull your arm through the sleeve now." Try for cooperation: "I've taken your sock halfway off—can you pull it the rest of the way?" Accept their feelings: "I know you don't like this, but we'll be finished in a minute." Talking to babies too young to understand may seem strange, but the understanding comes sooner than you realize—and it comes because you have been talking to the babies from the beginning.

You may also feel guilty doing something you enjoy—such as playing with a single baby—when you "should be working." Remember, you are working when you are playing with babies one at a time. You are doing very important work.

Mobile Infants

Although young infants generally lie still while being dressed, mobile infants (who are capable of cooperating) often try to get away. The trick is to contain them long enough to pull off a wet shirt or to put on a sweater to go outside. But the same principles still hold: Treat the infants with respect, try for cooperation, and accept their feelings.

You are likely to get more cooperation in undressing than in dressing; pulling off a hat or shoe is easier than putting one on. Realize that pulling off clothes is the first step, and even when it occurs at unplanned and unnecessary times, the infant is developing important skills. Babies do not pull clothes off to annoy

Dressing young infants may seem a little like dressing dolls.

you, they do it because they are practicing—unless you have made such a fuss in the past that they do it to get your attention. If that happens, be sure to stop making a fuss following undressing and start giving plenty of close attention to the child at other times. While you are living through the undressing period of some children, try to remember that dressing skills will eventually follow.

Mobile infants who are willing can easily push arms through armholes and legs into pants. They are probably interested in working on zippers that you have started if there is a big enough tab to grasp. They can untie shoes, but tying comes much later, as does buttoning and snapping. You can help the process by having available for practice dolls with easy-to-handle clothes and button boards or frames with a variety of fasteners, such as buttons, snaps, and hooks.

Older Infants

Older infants have increased dressing skills, and some children may be able to dress themselves if the clothes are simple and large enough. Most older infants, however, still need help. How much or little older infants cooperate depends on how willing they are. If they are in the stage of finding out the extent of their power to say no, they may well go in the opposite direction when you mention the need to change a shirt or put on a sweater.

Even when older infants are uncooperative, you must treat them with respect. After you catch them, you can explain that you see how negative they feel about changing but that the change is important for whatever reason: "I see you really don't want to put on your sweater, but it is too cold to go outside without it. I won't let you go outside without your sweater on." If you can give older infants an acceptable alternative, do so. Having a choice helps children feel more powerful: "You can stay in if you don't want to put your sweater on." "You have to change your shirt, but you can choose the red one or the blue one to change into."

A child's whole day may be ruined by having to wear a shirt that does not belong to him or her. (That is a good reason to have parents bring extra clothes.) Or an older infant new to the program may mightily resist taking a sweater off. The child may feel the stay is temporary if only he or she can manage to leave the sweater on. Perhaps the sweater gives the child comfort, like a security blanket. In such a case, it is probably worth letting the child leave the sweater on even if the child gets hot.

Dressing also gives the child opportunities for sensory experiences, both positive and negative. Some children dislike wearing short sleeves or short pants. Perhaps the air on their arms or legs makes them feel vulnerable. Other children find certain materials uncomfortable against their skin. Skin sensitivity varies. Imagine how you would suffer if a wool sweater made you itch and you could not take it off. Try to understand a child's sensitivities and strong opinions about clothes. You may not be able to go along with every whim, but if you make an effort to see things from the individual's point of view, you might find ways to be flexible about issues that really matter to the child. A child's personal preferences are often related to his or her temperament, such as a sensitivity to certain fabrics or the way clothes fit. For more information about temperaments, refer to the video *Flexible, Fearful, or Feisty: The Different Temperaments of Infants and Toddlers* and the article on temperamental differences in the book *Infant/Toddler Caregiving: A Guide to Social–Emotional Growth and Socialization.*

Although you always stress self-help skills, sometimes you have to weigh the need for competence against the need for nurturance. If an older infant says, "I can't; you do it" when sitting by the door with shoes in his or her hands, ordinarily you might say, "You put them on, and I'll tie them." But if the child is having a hard day or is ordinarily competent and self-sufficient, you might say, for a change, "I know you can do it, but I see you need me to do it for you this time."

In any routine making a smooth transition from other activities helps. It is very difficult for a child suddenly to be pulled

Sometimes you have to weigh the need for competence against the need for nurturance.

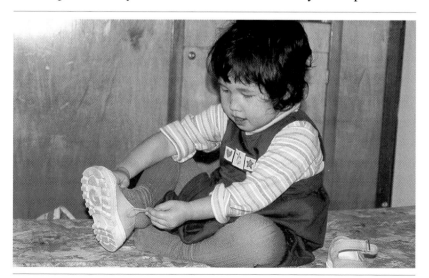

indoors from a happy time at the water table to have his or her clothes changed. A warning and a waiting period help: "I am going to have to change your clothes in a few minutes." Sometimes you can catch the child between activities: "I see you're finished washing your hands. Now I'm going to help you put on a dry shirt before we go in to snack."

When children are used to the idea that one event precedes or follows another, they get used to the routine (and most accept it). For example, children get used to taking off their shoes for naptime, which occurs after lunch. And they know that they put their coats on before going outside.

Your goals and philosophy more than likely reflect independence as a value. That is why you teach the self-help skills involved with dressing. However, it is important for you to remember that not all individuals or cultures value independence equally. Parents who teach *interdependence* rather than independence may not expect their children to dress themselves even though they are capable of it. The parents may not put any energy into teaching the children and, instead, may do everything for them. You need to recognize and respect the different viewpoints of those parents with regard to children dressing themselves. Most parents will not complain if you teach their children self-help skills. It is your responsibility to be equally respectful of how parents care for their children at home.

A word must be said about how much clothing to put on young children. Determine each baby's comfort zone. Some adults tend to dress children according to adult comfort levels, so they dress babies as they would want to be dressed. If adults' internal thermostats are similar to the babies', that will work. But temperature regulation is an individual matter, and some "cold-blooded" adults may overdress babies. In a very young infant, overheating may be a risk factor for sudden infant death syndrome (SIDS).

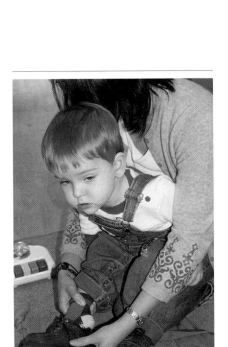

Parents who teach **interdependence** *rather than independence may not expect their children to dress themselves even though they are capable of it.*

Grooming

Grooming can be considered a part of dressing and is often done routinely after naps and before going home. It can also be done on an as-needed basis. Hand washing, of course, is not just for appearances and must be done throughout the day as a sanitation measure.

Periodically children need tidying up—faces and hands washed and hair combed. Because they get messy again so fast, it may not seem important to the caregiver to keep them well

groomed, especially those children who do not enjoy being cleaned or combed. However, some parents may have a different perspective on their children's appearance. They may be distressed to see their children with smeary faces or messy hair. It is too easy to discount those parents' strong feelings by saying they are putting too much importance on appearances when you do not understand why they feel so strongly. For example, they may feel their children look neglected if they are not properly groomed, which reflects on them, the parents. Pay attention to what distresses parents; do not ignore their wishes simply because they do not go along with what you believe is best for children.

Bathing

Bathtime can be a most enjoyable experience for both adult and child. It is another opportunity, as is dressing, for those one-to-one interactions that are so valuable to the child's development. Because this routine is so pleasurable, regular bathing probably should be left to the parent(s) unless you have a special reason to give baths in your program. More likely you will give an occasional bath when a child needs it for a special reason. Be aware, however, that even the occasional bath may tread on the parent's territory unless he or she is as convinced as you are that the child needed it.

Some cultures do not regard bathing as a daily necessity and believe that many North Americans overdo the practice. These differing views may cause conflicts. The baby seen by a parent as clean enough may not meet your standards. If you bathe the baby, the parent may take the action as a personal insult—a message that he or she is not taking good enough care of the child. Strong feelings may result from such a situation.

Or the parent may be on the other side of the conflict. Programs often provide sensory experiences that end up being quite messy—finger painting or sand and water play, for example. Parents may be distressed when they pick up their child and find him or her in less than the pristine condition in which they delivered the child that morning.

It does not take long to discover which parents have expectations of cleanliness. Respond to those expectations by cleaning the child as much as possible or by giving a bath if you have the facilities. Sand in cornrowed hair or stains on clothing may complicate the situation, however. If either of these is a concern of the parents, take steps to prevent such occurrences. Cover the child's clothes or remove them during messy activities. Stay by the child in the sandbox and protect the child. (Older infants need to be taught from the beginning not to throw sand—it gets in the eyes as well as in the hair.)

Young Infants

The following steps are for bathing very young infants:

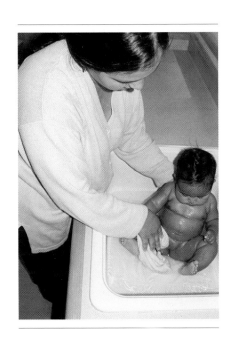

1. Make sure the room is warm enough.
2. Have all the supplies you will need at hand. These include tub, pad, mild soap, towel, clean diaper, and clothes. (Never leave a baby alone on a counter or in a tub while you get something you need.)
3. Half fill the baby bathtub with body-temperature water. (A plastic tub on a counter works well, or you can use a sink.) Test the water with your elbow or wrist. The water should feel warm but not hot.
4. Start with the infant's head. Wash the face with a soft cloth; do not use soap. Some people use sterile cotton instead of the washcloth for washing around the eyes. Clean the ears by using a corner of the washcloth and a finger. Do not stick cotton swabs in the infant's ears. If the hair is to be washed, wash it next by tucking the infant under your arm, supporting the head with one hand. Hold the head over the tub or under the faucet to wet the hair; soap up, rinse, and towel dry.

   Do not worry about touching the soft spot (fontanel) on the top of the baby's head. A tough membrane protects the brain, so you do not have to be extra careful. You can wash the area as you do the rest of the head.

5. There are two ways to give the rest of the bath. One is to do the washing on the pad outside the tub and to rinse the baby in the tub. The other is to put the infant in the tub, carefully supporting the head with one hand while you wash and rinse with the other. Use a cloth or just your hand. Be sure to wash and rinse all wrinkles and crevices.

6. Take the baby out of the tub, wrap him or her in a towel, and pat dry. Apply baby oil or cornstarch if you want to, although neither is really necessary. (Applying something to the infant's skin is a tradition rather than a biological necessity. During the application you can massage the infant for a while, which some adults and some babies enjoy.)

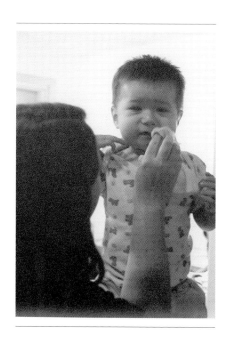

The steps are simple, but bathing a very young baby may not be. Some young babies scream when undressed, which may make bathtime difficult. The temptation is to bathe the baby as fast as possible to be rid of the task. There is nothing wrong with speed as long as you are still respectful in the way you treat the baby. As you do in diapering, dressing, and feeding, tell the baby what is going to happen every step of the way. Talk to the baby in soothing tones. Be gentle. Be responsive. The calmer and more relaxed you are, the better. Your calmness helps the infant settle down.

Mobile and Older Infants

Bathing mobile and older infants is easier in some ways than bathing very young infants; in other ways it is harder. Older babies and infants are not as delicate and slippery as younger ones, but they may be active and hard to control. They usually love water, but they may not like the washing part of a bath—especially getting their faces washed. Sometimes you can get children to wash themselves, which involves them even more fully in the process.

Some children, especially between the ages of one and two years, are fearful of bathing or hair washing or both. If fear is a problem, try changing the scene. Bathe children in a plastic tub if you have been using a regular bathtub or a sink. (Sometimes the water running down the drain scares children—they think they might slip down, too.) Use less water. Try sponge baths for a while. Water play in which the child has freedom to explore and experience the water on his or her own, at times other than bathtime, may help make bathing easier and less frightening.

The bathtub provides older infants not only pleasure but also learning experiences. Bathing is the ultimate water play. Children get a science lesson as they discover the properties of water. A few containers and maybe a sponge or two added to the bath water allow children to pour, dip, sink, float, and squeeze while they are bathing. Of course, you do not want to turn this time entirely into a play session—but it does not hurt if bathing is fun. Keeping in mind that bathing is a goal-oriented activity will keep you on the task.

When you are bathing older infants, safety is the primary concern. The following procedures are some ways to make bathtime safe and healthy:

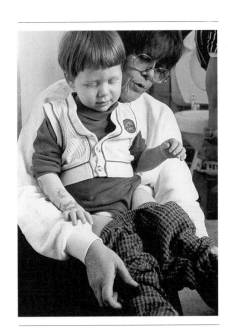

1. Never leave a child alone in the tub—not even for a moment. As with young infants, have everything you need at hand for the bath.
2. Always test the water to be sure it is not hot. Bad burns have resulted from adult carelessness about water temperature.
3. Make sure the bottom of the tub is not slippery. Use a rubber mat or nonskid stickers on the bottom.
4. Control the child's behavior in the tub if he or she tries to stand up or gets very active.
5. Use a clean washcloth and towel for each child.
6. Wash the tub thoroughly after each use.
7. Use fresh water for each child.

Points to Consider

1. What can be dangerous about washing and bathing? What precautions can you take to ensure the health and safety of each child you wash, bathe, or dress?
2. How can you make bathing or dressing a respectful experience if the child is crying, refusing, or exhibiting fear?
3. Are you aware of parents' feelings about having their children bathed away from home? Do you have some ideas for solving problems with those parents whose views may be in conflict with yours?
4. How can you make dressing, washing, and bathing more convenient for yourself and still take a respectful approach to each child?

Suggested Resources

Books and Articles

American Academy of Pediatrics, Committee on Infectious Diseases. *2000 Red Book Report of the Committee on Infectious Diseases* (24th edition). Elk Grove Village, Ill.: American Academy of Pediatrics, 2000.

The first new edition in three years advances the *Red Book*'s mission for the twenty-first century with the most current information on clinical manifestations, etiology, epidemiology, diagnosis, and treatment of more than 200 childhood infectious diseases. It was developed with the assistance and advice of hundreds of physician contributors from across the country. The new edition contains many significant revisions, updates, and additions to its authoritative content.

Caring for Our Children: National Health and Safety Performance Standards: Guidelines for Out-of-Home Child Care Programs. Prepared by American Public Health Association staff and American Academy of Pediatrics staff. Elk Grove Village, Ill.: American Academy of Pediatrics, 2000.

Contains guidelines on the health and safety needs of children from birth to twelve years in family and group child care homes and centers. It includes information on licensing, the child-to-staff ratio, emergency procedures, prevention and control of injury and infectious diseases, special needs, and so forth. Also contains information from the Consumer Product Safety Commission about crib safety.

Gerber, Magda. "Caring for Infants with Respect: The RIE Approach," *Zero to Three* (February 1984), 1–3.

Presents Magda Gerber's approach to caring for infants and toddlers: she recommends that caregivers always respect babies.

Gerber, Magda, and Allan Johnson. *Your Self-Confident Baby: How to Encourage Your Child's Natural Abilities from the Very Start.* New York: John Wiley & Sons, 1998.

Presents Gerber's philosophy of respect for the autonomy and competence of infants and toddlers in relation to all aspects of care, including feeding, diapering, and napping.

Gonzalez-Mena, Janet. *Multicultural Issues in Child Care* (Third edition). Mountain View, Calif.: Mayfield Publishing Co., 2001.

Explores cultural differences in beliefs, values, attitudes, approaches, and caregiving practices.

Gonzalez-Mena, Janet, and Dianne W. Eyer. *Infants, Toddlers, and Caregivers* (Fifth edition). Mountain View, Calif.: Mayfield Publishing Co., 2001.

Discusses caregiving routines, including dressing, that make up a major part of the child care curriculum.

Healthy Young Children: A Manual for Programs. Edited by A. S. Kendrick, R. Kaufman, and K. P. Messenger. Washington, D.C.: National Association for the Education of Young Children, 1995.

This basic manual is used in early childhood programs to promote the health and safety of children, staff, and families. Designed for ease in finding information, it is frequently used as a textbook.

Infant/Toddler Caregiving: A Guide to Social–Emotional Growth and Socialization. Sacramento: California Department of Education, 1990.

Presents information on temperaments and offers suggestions for caregiving.

Keeping Kids Healthy: Preventing and Managing Communicable Disease in Child Care. Sacramento: California Department of Education, 1995.

This manual is designed for use in child care settings with children from birth to five years. It contains chapters on understanding, preventing, recognizing, and managing communicable disease. A list of resources is included.

A Manual for Parents and Professionals. Edited by Magda Gerber. Los Angeles: Resources for Infant Educarers, 1978.

Explains how the RIE method works and gives practical advice about how to put respect into caregiving routines, such as dressing. Available from Resources for Infant Educarers (RIE), 1550 Murray Circle, Los Angeles, CA 90026.

Samuels, Mike, and Nancy Samuels. *The Well Baby Book.* New York: Summit Books, 1979.
Examines babies' needs and health issues from a holistic health perspective.

Setting Up for Infant/Toddler Care: Guidelines for Centers and Family Child Care Homes (Revised edition). Edited by Annabelle Godwin and Lorraine Schrag. Washington, D.C.: National Association for the Education of Young Children, 1996.

Includes practical information regarding business aspects of setting up a child care program. Experts describe how to promote all areas of a child's development.

Thoman, Evelyn B., and Sue Browder. *Born Dancing: The Relaxed Parents' Guide to Making Babies Smart with Love.* New York: Harper and Row, 1987.

Explores how babies communicate and describes how caregivers can trust, respect, and understand babies' unspoken language and natural rhythms, thus engaging in a dance with the infants.

Audiovisuals

Caring for Our Children. Elk Grove Village, Ill.: National Association for the Education of Young Children, 1995. Six 30-minute videocassettes.

The six videos show how to comply with the health and safety guidelines set forth in the manual of the same title. Each video clearly presents the appropriate steps to take to ensure safe and healthy out-of-home care.

Day Care: A Comprehensive Look—Infants and Toddlers (Part I). Tuckahoe, N.Y.: Campus Films Distributors Corp., 1979. Filmstrip, color, 90 slides; sound on cassette; printed guide.

Discusses the importance of attending to the total development of the child. Emphasizes the importance of daily routines as a time for children to learn and acquire good feelings about the world. Available from Campus Films Distributors Corp., 24 Depot Sq., Tuckahoe, NY 10707.

Flexible, Fearful, or Feisty: The Different Temperaments of Infants and Toddlers. Sacramento: California Department of

Education (with WestEd), 1990. Videocassette, color, 29 minutes; printed guide.

Identifies nine temperamental traits exhibited by infants and toddlers that are typically grouped into three temperamental types, described in the video as flexible, fearful, and feisty. Provides caregivers with techniques for dealing with the differences between individual infants and toddlers in group child care settings.

Getting in Tune: Creating Nurturing Relationships with Infants and Toddlers. Sacramento: California Department of Education (with WestEd), 1988. Videocassette, color, 24 minutes; printed guide.

Presents the "responsive process," which includes three steps: watching, asking, and adapting. Helps the caregiver learn what a young child needs and how best to respond to that need.

Respectfully Yours: Magda Gerber's Approach to Professional Infant/Toddler Care. Sacramento: California Department of Education (with WestEd), 1988. Videocassette, color, 55 minutes; printed guide.

Presents Magda Gerber's philosophy based on respecting the baby.

Information Hotline

California Child Care Health Line: 1-800-333-3212

This hotline provides child care health and safety information Monday through Thursday, 8 a.m. to 4 p.m.

Section Five:
Sleeping and Naptime

Rest needs vary greatly from the two-month-old to the three-year-old and from one individual to another, regardless of age. Most young infants need a good deal more sleep than do older infants. It is vital that young and mobile infants be allowed to establish and maintain their own sleeping schedules and not be expected to conform to a group schedule. For older infants (sixteen to thirty-six months), you can establish a regular afternoon naptime routine rather than continue the individual schedules for each child. However, the environment should be set up to allow those children to seek out soft, quiet, out-of-the-way spaces to rest whenever the need arises.

Young Infants

The primary requirements for meeting young infants' sleeping needs are a sensitive caregiver who can read each child's signals and a safe, comfortable, familiar place to sleep.

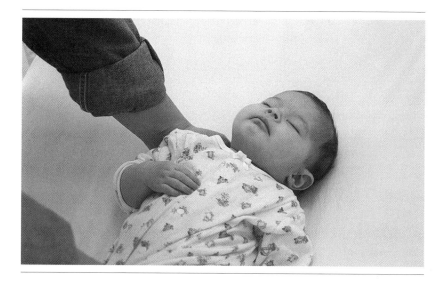

Most young infants need a good deal more sleep than do older infants.

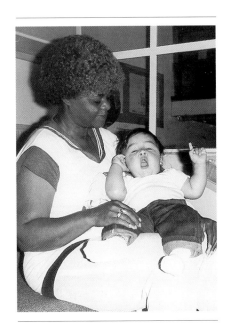

Safe means that infants should be put to sleep on their backs, particularly if they are under six months of age. This recommendation is a change from the previous recommendation of putting infants to sleep on their stomachs. Medical research has now determined that the risk of sudden infant death syndrome (SIDS) is greater if infants sleep on their stomachs. To prevent smothering, put young infants to sleep on a firm, smooth surface, not on a pillow, down comforter, sheepskin, or beanbag chair. Consider using a sleeper with no other coverings. If using a blanket, put the baby with his or her feet at the foot of the crib. Tuck a thin blanket around the crib mattress, only as far as the baby's chest. Make sure the baby's head remains uncovered during sleep.

Infants should not be placed in cribs unless they are ready to go to sleep. If you make a distinction between the place to play and the place to sleep, infants will go to sleep more easily. Nonmobile infants need to spend waking hours lying in safe places where they can look around, use their hands, kick their feet, and change positions freely. They should also be in close contact with their caregivers and other children. Appropriate places for awake, nonmobile infants are on the floor, in playpens, outside on a blanket on the grass, or in an open carriage under a tree—but not in a crib. An adult must take responsibility for noting when a child needs to sleep and put that child in his or her own crib.

Clues to Sleepiness

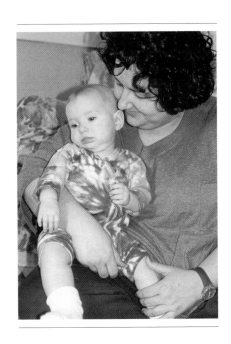

You can easily tell when young infants are sleepy if they yawn, rub their eyes, or drift off. But what about a baby who is screaming at the top of his or her lungs or fussing unhappily? How can you tell whether sleep is what the child needs?

One way to know is by what the parents tell you. Many parents are quite tuned in to their baby's individual cues and schedules. The parents know that the reason the baby cries about 10 a.m. is that the baby is tired. Maybe the baby was up most of the night. If you have that information in the morning, you will know that when the baby cries after drinking the bottle, the child is most likely sleepy. You will know that the most appropriate action is to put the baby in the crib and expect him or her to sleep.

What if the infant does not sleep but continues to cry? What do you do then? What you do depends again on your knowledge of that particular infant. Perhaps you have been told by the parent or know from experience that the baby needs to fuss for a few minutes before settling down to sleep. If that is the case, then the baby needs to stay in the crib and fuss. Or you may know that once a particular child starts crying, the child gets so worked up that he or she takes a long time to settle down to sleep. You will take that child out of the crib and find ways to relax and comfort the child until he or she can again be put down to sleep. Perhaps you know (from the parents or from experience) that this particular baby goes to sleep faster if rocked. In that case you will rock the baby.

During the transition from being awake to falling asleep, trust is important. Trust, which allows children to let go and fall asleep, develops most easily with a primary caregiver system. This system encourages attachment to one special caregiver and supports the development of trust. Thus at sleeping times, when children often feel the most vulnerable, they are able to relax because their primary caregiver knows and is part of their individual presleep ritual.

The Right Environment

The first requirement for meeting young infants' sleeping needs is a primary caregiver who can read the children's signals and who knows each child's routine. The second requirement is a safe, comfortable, familiar place to sleep. The younger the infant, the more likely that a small, confined area, such as a bassinet or a baby carriage, will provide a sense of security. Some young infants fear wide open spaces, and even a crib feels unsafe to them. After a few months, the size of the space becomes less of a problem. Of course, a baby should never be placed in a bassinet

The transition from being awake to falling asleep is a time when trust is important.

or carriage if there is even the slightest chance that he or she may pull up, roll over, or fall out. Young infants may also be stimulated by the views a crib affords of other cribs and babies. Sleeping under those circumstances may be difficult. Crib bumpers can cut down on visual stimulation for infants and can provide comfort for young infants who sometimes squirm up to the crib slats as they sleep; however, they can also be dangerous. If crib bumpers are soft or frilly, they can entrap tiny infants. Be sure bumpers have an intact covering, are firm and tightly fitting, and have no strings. Because views are no longer hidden by bumpers when infants graduate from a crib to cot or mat, visual stimulation may remain an issue through the older infant years. Organizing care in small groups, placing cots and mats as far away from each other as possible, and using screens to block children's view of one another are ways of addressing this problem.

Colors in sleeping areas should be toned down—soft colors and earth tones are best. The bright reds, yellows, and oranges sometimes found in infant care environments may be overstimulating anywhere, but especially in the sleeping areas. Avoid exciting, interesting pictures, toys, and other visual enticements as well, and keep noise to a minimum.

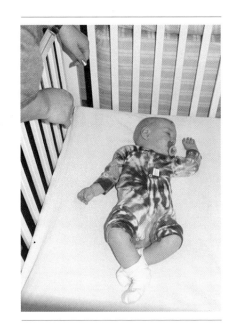

Some cultures view outdoor sleeping as healthier than indoor sleeping. Child care programs in some countries have outdoor sleeping areas for summer and sleeping porches with screens instead of windows for winter. Although such setups are rare or nonexistent in this country, some caregivers who value fresh air do find ways for the youngest infants to sleep outdoors in baby carriages. There is nothing like a slight breeze moving the leaves of a tree above to help the baby in a carriage go to sleep in a few minutes.

Safety considerations are vital when providing for sleeping needs. Never put an infant to bed with a propped bottle; infants have choked because of bottles. Avoid soft cushions or pillows that infants can get wedged under. Use only safety-approved cribs, bassinets, and carriages with properly fitting mattresses. All cribs should be child-proofed before they are used. Inspect the crib or cot to be sure there are no gaps between the mattress and the sides where arms and legs might get caught. The minimum rail height should be 22 inches from the top of the railing to the top of the mattress when the rail is set at the lowest level. Slats should be no more than $2\frac{3}{8}$ inches apart. Wood surfaces should be free of splinters and cracks and have lead-free paint. The sides should be at least 4 inches above the mattress when in

The following tips may help in putting older infants down for a nap:

1. Make sure that the older infants in the program get plenty of fresh air and exercise every day. There is nothing like being tired to provide motivation for going to sleep. However, be careful children do not get overtired. Some older infants have a very hard time settling down to sleep when overtired.

2. Provide a transition period between active play and sleep. Many programs serve lunch right before naptime, providing a change of pace. After lunch and cleanup, children take off their shoes and may be undressed. (Not all programs change clothes for sleeping.) These routines provide clues about what is to come and prepare the children to settle down.

3. Change the setting. Put toys away, preferably in closed cabinets. The cots that occupy the playspace are a reminder that naptime is approaching. Toward the end of the transition, the lights are usually turned down or the shades are pulled. In some programs soft music is played, thus providing a more relaxed atmosphere than the earlier bright, toy-filled setting.

4. If some children have difficulty lying down for a nap, care for them in a separate area while the children who nap more easily are settled into their beds. Then you will be free to help those who need more time and attention to wind down.

5. Learn which rituals work best with which children. Some children are used to hearing a story before going to sleep. Others are sung to. Some enjoy a back rub, which soothes and relaxes them. Many children have a favored object or blanket they take to bed with them. Getting the object and snuggling down with it can be part of the ritual.

Temperamental Differences

Some infants establish regular schedules and are easy to put down to sleep. Others have irregular schedules, are less predictable, and may have difficulty going to sleep. Both types of children need to be helped to take a nap when they are tired, even if they protest.

Some infants are soothed by rocking, rubbing, or being sung to. However, some highly sensitive infants are stimulated rather than soothed by voices, rubbing, or even the presence of other people when trying to go to sleep.

Some infants are more persistent than others in their protests about going to sleep. Do not leave a child to cry for long periods, but do stand firm if sleep is what is needed. Periodically you may

Try to be sensitive to different styles of waking up.

gently reassure the child that he or she is not alone, but do not give up on putting the child to sleep.

Waking-up Styles

Some children take long naps; others take shorter ones. You can meet individual needs by setting up a place for the short nappers to go to so they will not disturb the longer nappers. Some programs send children outside when they wake up (in good weather). Other programs have a room children can go to or an area of the room set up for the early risers.

Children wake up in different moods and degrees of readiness for interaction. Some are slow wakers and need a long transition to lie around and get fully awake. The presence of the primary caregiver is especially helpful for these children. Other children bounce up and are ready to resume where they left off playing. Knowing and responding to each child's style and needs at wake-up time is an important part of infant/toddler care.

Children Who Have Difficulty Sleeping

Some children have a harder time than others sleeping in the child care setting. You can tell by knowing the child whether the child is tired and needs a nap or simply is not ready at the time. If the child is particularly fussy or easily frustrated, the chances are the child is tired but having a difficult time winding down or letting him- or herself go to sleep.

Consult with parents about their children's sleeping habits and patterns at the very beginning of the enrollment period so that you can make napping as much like the routine at home as possible.

Trust is an important factor in children's ability to fall asleep. Establishing a naptime ritual with a primary caregiver the child knows and trusts can transform a "difficult napper" into one who looks forward to the routine. With a child who is new to the program, however, the prompt assignment of a primary caregiver will set the stage for trust to develop, but the child may not feel comfortable enough to nap right away. A transitional object, such as a special toy or a blanket, may help; if not, as in any instance where children do not sleep during the regular naptime, the child will need a separate area with a choice of activities. If the primary caregiver can be with the child at this time, it will provide a valuable opportunity for the two to get to know each other and begin to bond.

If the child has trouble napping once the adjustment period is over, ask family members whether they have an idea about what is causing it or any suggestions for what to do about it. Something may be happening at home that is different from what the child is used to, such as a change in schedule or a new baby in the family, which is creating unusual stress in the child.

Overstimulation in the program can also prevent children from relaxing into needed sleep, especially if they are highly sensitive or distractible. Begin with transitional activities that are peaceful, so that children have a chance to wind down from their play. The napping environment may also be a problem. The child may need more isolation than you have been providing; a change in the setting, such as using a screen to cut down on visual stimulation, may help. Following individual children's napping needs rather than enforcing a universal naptime can also make naptime easier because it cuts down on the number of children who are trying to go to sleep at one time. Children who are not ready for sleep often disturb those who are tired.

A child's difficulty in going to sleep may be due to a habit that the child has developed of refusing to nap in order to get attention. If the child's need for attention is the reason for the behavior, it is important to be calm in responding to the child's refusal to rest and to give the child extra attention at other times.

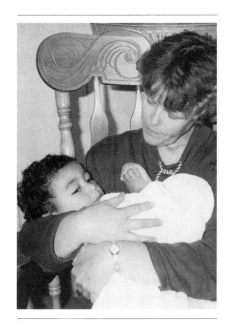

In general, however, if you are certain that the child is tired, the environment is appropriate for napping, and the child still has trouble lying down, it will help to sit next to the child to encourage him or her to stay on the cot or mat. In a friendly but firm tone, state that you know the child is tired and that you are going to stay nearby to help him or her get the nap he or she needs. Getting upset will wake the child even more. Try different techniques until you find one that soothes the child, such as humming or singing, patting the child's back, stroking the head, and so forth. A tired child with a familiar routine and a caregiver with whom he or she has a close relationship will rarely be difficult to get down to nap, although it may take some time and patience.

A few children between the ages of two and three years are ready to give up naptime. Although most older infants will fall asleep if they spend some time on their cots, programs must have a plan for children who do not need naps at all as well as for children who nap at different times from the rest. In a separate area, provide a few choices of interesting, quiet activities and take advantage of the low child–adult ratio to give the child special attention. Do not make a child feel bad about himself or herself because of biological rhythms that are different from those of other children. When the environment and staffing patterns are set up to accommodate children who do not sleep, it is easier to be positive and supportive of their individuality.

Working with Parents Around Nap Routines

The situation is more complicated when the parents' ideas about naptime are different from those of the staff. Some parents believe it is important not to enforce naptime, preferring that their children learn to read their own body signs and rest when they are tired rather than according to the schedule. Other parents may have had difficulties getting their children to bed at night when the children have a long nap in the afternoon. Parents' scheduling needs may not mesh easily with the staff schedule or even with the child's need for sleep in child care. The parents may request either that you not put the child down at all or that you wake the child up after a set amount of time.

Unless you feel you can simply do what the parent asks without harm or discomfort to the child, there are no easy solutions to these issues. The four-step process recommended in the video *Protective Urges: Working with the Feelings of Parents and Caregivers* may help caregivers sort out the issues and come up with a satisfactory resolution.

For example, a father asks you to wake his infant from a nap. You feel the child needs the sleep. Every day you tell the father why you couldn't wake the child: she is especially tired, has hurt herself, or is ill. You feel nervous when the father arrives. He avoids eye contact and doesn't speak. What can you do? Step 1, explore what you are feeling and why. Are you worried or resentful? Were you brought up to think of sleep as sacred and never to be interrupted? Step 2, check out your feelings with your co-worker, who thinks you are overreacting because you are so close to the child. Step 3, approach the father, not to solve the problem but to learn about his point of view. He is working and studying full time. He can't study at night because the baby is awake. Step 4, make a plan. For instance, you will get more physical exercise to help you with life's stresses. You will meet with the father again and offer to put the child down for a nap earlier. You continue to work with the father toward a solution.

Recording the Information

How long their child slept and the time of the most recent awakening may be important information for parents who need to plan the evening with their children. Is the baby likely to be ready

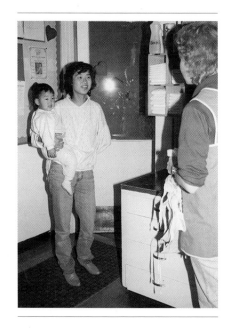

Parents and caregivers may have to work together toward a mutually acceptable solution to resolve conflicts over naptime schedules.

for bed soon after dinner or has the child been asleep all afternoon? Did the older infant wake up early from the nap? Is that why he or she is sleepy in the car going home? Napping information can be recorded easily in the same manner as feeding and diapering information. When there is consistency of caregivers and good communication, oral reporting is all that is necessary. If you are the primary caregiver, have a good memory, and are the one who delivers the baby into the arms of the parent, you can simply tell the parent how well the baby napped that day. But using memory alone means you do not have records over a period of time to note patterns and changes in those patterns, which can sometimes be helpful information.

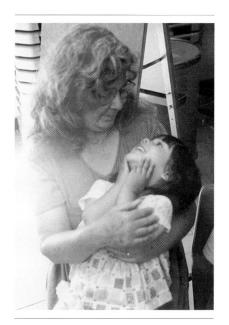

Points to Consider

1. How individualized are your napping routines? Do you allow infants and toddlers to set their own schedules? Does every child have at least one caregiver who knows his or her unique going-to-sleep and waking-up patterns? If the primary caregiver is not present, is there still consistency in the way the child is put to sleep?

2. How much thought have you given to setting up a safe, cozy, comfortable, and peaceful napping environment for each child?

3. Are the napping routines in child care consistent with the sleeping routines at home? What kind of communication do you have with parents about the child's sleeping needs and napping routines? What process do you have for problem solving in parent–caregiver disagreements over napping issues?

4. How well do the napping routines work for the caregivers in the program?

5. Do the napping routines fit into the overall program structure and philosophy?

Suggested Resources

Books and Articles

American Academy of Pediatrics. "Back to Sleep Campaign." Bethesda, Md.: National Institute of Child Health and Human Development, 1998.

Brochures, posters, crib stickers, door hangers, and videos convey information on safe sleeping practices for infants.

Most materials are available in English and Spanish. To order, write to the institute at 31 Center Drive, Room 2A32, Bethesda, MD 20892-2425; telephone (301) 435-3459 or 1-800-505-CRIB.

Another source of information, including brochures, is the California SIDS Program, Maternal Child Health Services; telephone (916) 536-0146.

American Academy of Pediatrics, Committee on Infectious Diseases. *2000 Red Book Report of the Committee on Infectious Diseases* (24th edition). Elk Grove Village, Ill.: American Academy of Pediatrics, 2000.

The first new edition in three years advances the *Red Book*'s mission for the twenty-first century with the most current information on clinical manifestations, etiology, epidemiology, diagnosis, and treatment of more than 200 childhood infectious diseases. It was developed with the assistance and advice of hundreds of physician contributors from across the country. The new edition contains many significant revisions, updates, and additions to its authoritative content.

Caring for Our Children: National Health and Safety Performance Standards: Guidelines for Out-of-Home Child Care Programs. Prepared by American Public Health Association staff and American Academy of Pediatrics staff. Elk Grove Village, Ill.: American Academy of Pediatrics, 2000.

Contains guidelines on the health and safety needs of children from birth to twelve years in family and group child care homes and centers. It includes information on licensing, the child-to-staff ratio, emergency procedures, prevention and control of injury and infectious diseases, special needs, and so forth. Also contains information from the Consumer Product Safety Commission about crib safety.

Ferber, Richard, M.D. *Solve Your Child's Sleep Problems.* New York: Simon & Schuster, 1985.

Based on research, this book offers practical tips for addressing sleep issues associated with children aged one to six, including refusal to go to bed, colic and other medical problems, restlessness, insomnia, night terrors, and bed wetting. Contains a bibliography of children's "go-to-sleep" books.

Gerber, Magda. "Caring for Infants with Respect: The RIE Approach," *Zero to Three* (February 1984), 1–3.

Presents Magda Gerber's approach to caring for infants and toddlers: she recommends that caregivers always respect babies.

Gerber, Magda and Allan Johnson. *Your Self-Confident Baby: How to Encourage Your Child's Natural Abilities from the Very Start.* New York: John Wiley & Sons, 1998.

Presents Gerber's philosophy of respect for the autonomy and competence of infants and toddlers in relation to all aspects of care, including daily routines.

Gonzalez-Mena, Janet. *Multicultural Issues in Child Care* (Third edition). Mountain View, Calif.: Mayfield Publishing Co., 2001.

Explores some cultural differences in beliefs, values, attitudes, approaches, and practices related to sleeping.

Gonzalez-Mena, Janet. *Tips and Tidbits: A Book for Family Child Care Providers.* Washington, D.C.: National Association for the Education of Young Children, 1991.

Offers ideas for handling eating or napping difficulties, squabbling, "potty mouth," and other day-to-day matters that arise in a child care provider's life.

Gonzalez-Mena, Janet, and Dianne W. Eyer. *Infants, Toddlers, and Caregivers* (Fifth edition). Mountain View, Calif.: Mayfield Publishing Co., 2001.

Discusses caregiving routines that make up a major part of the child care curriculum.

Healthy Young Children: A Manual for Programs. Edited by A. S. Kendrick, R. Kaufman, and K. P. Messenger. Washington, D.C.: National Association for the Education of Young Children, 1995.

This basic manual is used in early childhood programs to promote the health and safety of children, staff, and families. Designed for ease in finding information, it is frequently used as a textbook.

Keeping Kids Healthy: Preventing and Managing Communicable Disease in Child Care. Sacramento: California Department of Education, 1994.

This manual is designed for use in child care settings with children from birth to five years. It contains chapters on understanding, preventing, recognizing, and managing communicable disease. A list of resources is included.

Leavitt, Robin L., and Brenda K. Eheart. "Managing Routines Within the Daily Schedule," in *Toddler Day Care: A Guide to Responsive Caregiving.* Lexington, Mass.: Lexington Books, 1985, pp. 51–52.

Provides ideas on how to help older infants make the transition to naptime and considers the issue of flexibility and sleeping schedules.

A Manual for Parents and Professionals. Edited by Magda Gerber. Los Angeles: Resources for Infant Educarers, 1978.

Explains how the RIE method works and gives practical advice about how to put respect into caregiving routines, such as napping and sleeping. Available from Resources for Infant Educarers (RIE), 1550 Murray Circle, Los Angeles, CA 90026.

Samuels, Mike, and Nancy Samuels. *The Well Baby Book.* New York: Summit Books, 1979.

Examines babies' needs and health issues from a holistic health perspective.

Setting Up for Infant/Toddler Care: Guidelines for Centers and Family Child Care Homes (Revised edition). Edited by Annabelle Godwin and Lorraine Schrag. Washington, D.C.: National Association for the Education of Young Children, 1996.

Includes practical information regarding business aspects of setting up a child care program. Experts describe how to promote all areas of a child's development.

Thoman, Evelyn B., and Sue Browder. *Born Dancing: The Relaxed Parents' Guide to Making Babies Smart with Love.* New York: Harper and Row, 1987.

Explores how babies communicate and describes how caregivers can trust, respect, and understand babies' unspoken language and natural rhythms, thus engaging in a dance with the infants.

Audiovisuals

Caring for Our Children. Elk Grove Village, Ill.: American Academy of Pediatrics, 1995. Six 30-minute videotapes.

The six videos show how to comply with the health and safety guidelines set forth in the manual of the same title. Each video clearly presents the appropriate steps to take to ensure safe and healthy out-of-home care.

Flexible, Fearful, or Feisty: The Different Temperaments of Infants and Toddlers. Sacramento: California Department of Education (with WestEd), 1990. Videocassette, color, 29 minutes; printed guide.

Identifies nine temperamental traits exhibited by infants and toddlers that are typically grouped into three temperamental types, described in the video as flexible, fearful, and feisty. Provides caregivers with techniques for dealing with the differences between individual infants and toddlers in group child care settings.

Getting in Tune: Creating Nurturing Relationships with Infants and Toddlers. Sacramento: California Department of Education (with WestEd), 1988. Videocassette, color, 24 minutes; printed guide.

Presents the "responsive process," which includes three steps: watching, asking, and adapting. Helps the caregiver learn what a young child needs and how best to respond to that need.

It's Not Just Routine: Feeding, Diapering, and Napping Infants and Toddlers (Second edition). Sacramento: California Department of Education (with WestEd), 2000. Videocassette, color, 24 minutes; printed guide.

Updated version of the video demonstrates how to carry out sleeping and napping routines with infants and toddlers, including SIDS prevention and universal precautions. Particular attention is given to the setting and the quality of the experience for the child and the caregiver.

Respectfully Yours: Magda Gerber's Approach to Professional Infant/Toddler Care. Sacramento: California Department of Education (with WestEd), 1988. Videocassette, color, 55 minutes; printed guide.

Presents Magda Gerber's philosophy based on respecting the baby.

Information Hotline

California Child Care Health Line: 1-800-333-3212

This hotline provides child care health and safety information Monday through Thursday, 8 a.m. to 4 p.m.

Section Six:
Preparing, Ordering, and Maintaining the Environment

lanning and keeping an appropriate environment is an ongoing caregiver task. The environment should be set up for various activities during the day, flexible enough to meet individual needs, and changed on a regular basis, when necessary. In the early morning, you can set up cushions and pillows and cozy corners and expect snuggling and "reading" activities to take precedence over more active play. Later, breakfast routines will change the environment. After breakfast, most programs encourage free play, which usually involves more gross motor activity on the part of the children. Throughout the day, routines dictate the setup of the environment unless, of course, you have a different room for each routine.

Periodically check to be sure the environment is safe, sanitary, and developmentally appropriate. *Developmentally appropriate* means you have the right kinds of toys and equipment for the age group served. Most programs have a daily safety and sanitary check. The developmental appropriateness of the environment should be checked weekly for young and mobile infants and monthly for older infants. When new children enter the program, give immediate attention to the newcomers' developmental needs.

Children's Involvement

Keeping the environment clean and in good order is an ongoing caregiving routine, one in which you want to keep the children involved. Children pick up attitudes very quickly. If you are convinced that the responsibility is theirs as well as yours, they will be too. But if you approach cleanup with a negative attitude, children are likely to be uninterested in participating. If you make cleaning up interesting and fun, they do not see it as a chore but as a chance to get involved in helping you.

The age of the child influences how much help he or she will be. Children, even from a young age, can begin to develop some sense of responsibility for the environment they inhabit. Young infants, of course, will only watch the proceedings. But mobile infants are good imitators, and if you start putting toys on the shelves or balls back into a basket, you are likely to get cooperation from some "helpers." Older infants can be even more useful, matching toys to their pictures on the shelves and sorting bean bags from balls.

Order and Freedom

It is important that the environment is organized but not so organized that the children are discouraged from exploring. There is a delicate balance between maintaining order and giving freedom.

Obviously children cannot explore a puzzle if the pieces are scattered to the distant corners of the room. Beginning walkers cannot navigate a rug so littered with toys that they cannot find a space to put a foot. But young crawlers need a few interesting toys scattered around to motivate them to move around the room. If you keep order with too heavy a hand, either the children will be too inhibited or unmotivated to explore or they will make a game of destroying the order that you are pushing on them.

Children, even from a young age, can begin to develop some sense of responsibility for the environment they inhabit.

The nature of the activities that mobile and older infants engage in makes maintaining order hard. One such activity is dumping. A bucket or basket of objects invites dumping. The child may also refill the container, in which case the activity becomes a cycle: a dump–fill cycle. The problem is that because the activity is a cycle, the child is as likely to dump again as to put the container back on the shelf. If the child happens to grow tired of the activity at the end of the fill part of the cycle, you are lucky, but the chances are that the child will wander off after the last dump rather than the last fill, unless your timing is superb and you intervene.

Another activity common to mobile and older infants is pick up–carry–drop. When children begin to move around, they like to take objects with them. For instance, if you watch fourteen-month-olds, you will see that they often have in their hands objects that they drop or place on the floor in order to pick up another object. While charting this behavior, you may discover that a child may pick up, carry around, and put down as many as 20 objects in 15 minutes. That means if you are trying to keep everything in its place when it is not being played with, you are going to have a hard time—and so are the children.

Pickup Time

A more realistic goal is to control the number of toys and other objects put out at any time so that the environment is safe and interesting but not pristinely tidy. The toys are put back in place on the shelves periodically throughout the day during what is known as "pickup time." The event to follow is usually

If you include children in cleanup, regarding them as partners from the beginning, you may find that the job takes longer to get done. But the extra time at the beginning is an investment that pays off later.

exciting enough (such as going outside, going for a walk, having lunch) that children pick up toys in eager anticipation.

Children, especially older infants, can be involved in more of the cleanup routine than just picking up toys. Older infants can clear the table after lunch, deposit the dishes in an available container, and even wipe off their places at the table. Getting the children to do this takes some teaching and modeling, but if your directions are clear and simple, most older infants enjoy not only the responsibility but also the sensory aspects that go along with cleanup. (Using a dish cloth or wet paper towel may be a satisfying activity to older infants. Sponges are not recommended because they are often full of germs.)

Extent of Involvement

How involved the children are in preparing the environment depends on the program. Participation in routines is a major part of the curriculum for infants and toddlers. Some programs have a period to arrange and set things up before the children arrive for the day. Others are set up so that caregivers arrive with the children. In that case arranging equipment and setting out toys and activities may involve the children who arrive early unless the task is done by the last person to leave at night.

If you include children in cleanup, regarding them as partners from the beginning, you may find that the job takes longer to get done. But the extra time at the beginning is an investment that pays off later. Once children have gained skills, they become effective helpers who can save you time and effort.

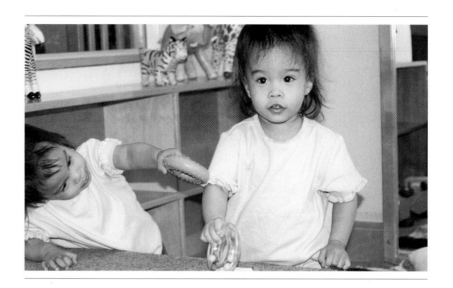

Setup and Maintenance

The following tips are for setting up and maintaining an orderly environment that invites exploration:

1. Provide low open shelves to store available toys. Put heavier toys on the lowest shelves. If you label (with pictures) the places for each toy, older infants can not only put the toys back in the right place but also work on a cognitive task (matching an object to a symbol) while they are doing so.

2. Select a number of toys that allow plenty to do but do not put out every toy. It is always a good practice to keep supplementary toys in closed cupboards that children cannot reach. Rotating some toys now and then keeps the environment interesting for the children.

3. Do not let disorder get beyond the capabilities of the "picker-uppers." Do regular pickup when needed rather than wait until lunch time. Even a moderately messy room may be overwhelming to older infants who want to help pick up. If too much of a mess has accumulated, break the activity down to manageable parts, saying, for example, "Let's put all the connecting blocks back in the can" instead of "Let's pick up the toys now."

4. Clean up one thing before starting another activity. Sometimes timing is such that you cannot quite manage that, but the day does go smoother if you have cleared away the finger paints before you start the lunch preparations.

5. Be cheerful and positive. Make a game of picking up. Your attitude is important, as is your presence. You cannot tell older infants to pick up and expect they will do it while you

turn to another task. You need to be involved, too. Your involvement is part of what makes the activity interesting to them. Picking up is a joint project—not the children's responsibility alone.

The video *Space to Grow: Creating a Child Care Environment for Infants and Toddlers* and the publication *Infant/Toddler Caregiving: A Guide to Setting Up Environments* provide many ideas on how to set up and maintain an orderly, effective environment for young infants, mobile infants, and older infants.

Sanitation Procedures

The sanitary aspects of cleanup necessarily exclude children's help because of the germs and chemicals involved. Because diseases such as hepatitis and giardia are on the increase, sanitation is essential to everyone's health. The following recommended routines will help prevent the spread of illness:

1. Keep floors clean: vacuum rugs daily; sweep and mop floors daily or after meals, when necessary; clean up spills as they occur.

2. Do not allow outside shoes to be worn in areas where infants lie or crawl. Soft, washable slippers with nonskid soles are recommended for caregivers. Or leave shoes on and cover them with surgical booties.

3. Wash toys and equipment as needed and at least once or twice daily. Use soap and water if toys are sticky or dirty, followed by a bleach solution. If there are no signs of dirt, use a bleach solution alone. Some programs' staff regularly run plastic toys through the dishwasher.

4. Use the sanitary diapering procedures outlined in "Diapering and Toileting."

5. Carefully wash bottles and eating utensils and sanitize them with a bleach solution or in a dishwasher with extra hot water.

6. Store bottles and opened or prepared food in the refrigerator at all times. Date items that go in so you can keep track of what is old.

7. Change bed linens once a week or immediately when soiled. See also Section Seven, "Health and Safety."

Safety Procedures

Safety is as important as sanitation. Some safety guidelines are as follows:

1. Cover all electrical outlets within the children's reach.

2. Remove all dangling cords and strings.

3. Formulate a plan in case of fire. Be sure all exit doors are clear. Organize a system for getting all children out. Install smoke detectors, fire alarms, and fire extinguishers and provide fire blankets for every child-care room.

4. All glass within the reach of children (windows, mirrors, aquariums, etc.) should be shatterproof or protected.

5. Find out which houseplants are poisonous (many are) and remove them.

6. Check outdoors for poisonous plants and remove them.

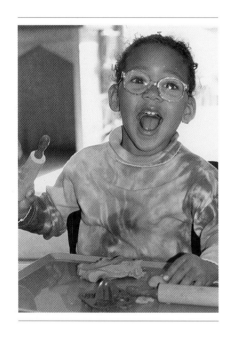

7. Keep all equipment in good repair and check regularly.

8. Use barriers around all heaters to prevent children from burn accidents.

9. Keep all cleaning supplies, medicines, and the staff's personal belongings away from the children. Those materials need to be locked away so children cannot possibly get to them.

10. Make sure all toys and equipment are age-appropriate for the children in the environment. Infants and toddlers should not have access to small objects, toys and toy parts less than $1^1/_4$ inches in diameter, coins, safety pins, marbles, plastic bags, balloons, Styrofoam objects that they can choke on, or objects with sharp points and edges. Climbing equipment must be at a safe height (a general rule is one foot per year of the child) and should be on appropriately soft surfaces.

11. Put gates across stairways and avoid the use of walkers.

12. Do not smoke in child care areas.

No matter how well the environment is set up, the most important safety measure is attentive adult supervision.

Points to Consider

1. Do your cleanup routines reflect the philosophy and goals of your program?
2. Are health and safety considerations part of your cleanup routine?
3. Do you make provisions for children to participate in cleanup at the appropriate developmental level of involvement?
4. How do you decide among staff what standards of orderliness are acceptable to all? Do you have a problem-solving process to work on conflicts?

Suggested Resources

Books and Articles

American Academy of Pediatrics, Committee on Infectious Diseases. *2000 Red Book Report of the Committee on Infectious Diseases* (24th edition). Elk Grove Village, Ill.: American Academy of Pediatrics, 2000.

The first new edition in three years advances the *Red Book*'s mission for the twenty-first century with the most current information on clinical manifestations, etiology, epidemiology, diagnosis, and treatment of more than 200 childhood infectious diseases. It was developed with the assistance and advice of hundreds of physician contributors from across the country. The new edition contains many significant revisions, updates, and additions to its authoritative content.

Caring for Our Children: National Health and Safety Performance Standards: Guidelines for Out-of-Home Child Care Programs. Prepared by American Public Health Association staff and American Academy of Pediatrics staff. Elk Grove Village, Ill.: American Academy of Pediatrics, 2000.

Contains guidelines on the health and safety needs of children from birth to twelve years in family and group child care homes and centers. It includes information on licensing, the child-to-staff ratio, emergency procedures, prevention and control of injury and infectious diseases, special needs, and so forth. Also contains information from the Consumer Product Safety Commission about crib safety.

Ferguson, J. "Creating Growth-Producing Environments for Infants and Toddlers," in *Supporting the Growth of Infants, Toddlers, and Parents.* Edited by E. Jones. Pasadena, Calif.: Pacific Oaks College, 1979, pp. 13–26.

Provides an overview of vital concerns in creating an environment for infants and toddlers.

Gonzalez-Mena, Janet. *Multicultural Issues in Child Care* (Third edition). Mountain View, Calif.: Mayfield Publishing Co., 2001.

Explores cultural differences in beliefs, values, attitudes, approaches, and caregiving practices.

Gonzalez-Mena, Janet, and Dianne W. Eyer. *Infants, Toddlers, and Caregivers* (Fifth edition). Mountain View, Calif.: Mayfield Publishing Co., 2001.

Discusses environments from the point of view of caregiving, free play, health, and safety.

Greenman, J. "Babies Get Out," *Beginnings* (Summer 1985).

Explores the value of taking infants and toddlers outdoors and offers practical suggestions on how to enhance outdoor experiences for young children.

Greenman, J. *Caring Spaces, Learning Places: Children's Environments That Work.* Redmond, Wash.: Exchange Press, 1988.

Discusses how to design and redesign center places and spaces for children and adults.

Healthy Young Children: A Manual for Programs. Edited by A. S. Kendrick, R. Kaufman, and K. P. Messenger. Washington, D.C.: National Association for the Education of Young Children, 1995.

This basic manual is used in early childhood programs to promote the health and safety of children, staff, and families. Designed for ease in finding information, it is frequently used as a textbook.

Infant/Toddler Caregiving: A Guide to Setting Up Environments. Sacramento: California Department of Education (with WestEd), 1990.

Presents ideas and suggestions for setting up and maintaining a rich, age-appropriate environment for infants and toddlers. Includes many photographs and illustrations.

Keeping Kids Healthy: Preventing and Managing Communicable Disease in Child Care. Sacramento: California Department of Education, 1995.

This manual is designed for use in child care settings with children from birth to five years. It contains chapters on

understanding, preventing, recognizing, and managing communicable disease. A list of resources is included.

Olds, A. R. "Designing Play Environments for Children Under
Three," *Topics in Early Childhood Special Education,* Vol. 2
(1982), 87–95.

Discusses what to consider when designing environments
for infants and toddlers.

*Setting Up for Infant/Toddler Care: Guidelines for Centers and
Family Child Care Homes* (Revised edition). Edited by
Annabelle Godwin and Lorraine Schrag. Washington, D.C.:
National Association for the Education of Young Children,
1996.

Includes practical information regarding business aspects of
setting up a child care program. Experts describe how to
promote all areas of a child's development.

Willis, Anne, and Henry Ricciuti. *A Good Beginning for Babies:
Guidelines for Group Care.* Washington, D.C.: National Association for the Education of Young Children, 1975.

Includes guidelines on physical space, equipment, health,
and safety.

Audiovisuals

Caring for Our Children. Elk Grove Village, Ill.: National
Association for the Education of Young Children, 1995. Six
30-minute videocassettes.

The six videos show how to comply with the health and safety
guidelines set forth in the manual of the same title. Each video
clearly presents the appropriate steps to take to ensure safe
and healthy out-of-home care.

*Space to Grow: Creating a Child Care Environment for Infants
and Toddlers.* Sacramento: California Department of Education (with WestEd), 1988. Videocassette, color, 22 minutes;
printed guide.

Discusses setting up and maintaining a rich, age-appropriate
environment for infants and toddlers.

Information Hotline

California Child Care Health Line: 1-800-333-3212

This hotline provides child care health and safety information
Monday through Thursday, 8 a.m. to 4 p.m.

Section Seven: Health and Safety

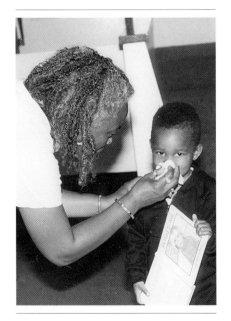

ealth and safety are serious matters that need to be attended to during all daily routines. When the routines are carried out with proper attention to health and safety, children and caregivers are healthier and happier. Families, too, will be reassured by the care taken to protect their children and the consistency with which health and safety policies are implemented. All parents and staff in your program should have current copies of your policy guidelines. Emergency information for contacting parents should be posted by the telephone for easy access.

Clearly defined and up-to-date written health and safety policies are important for your program. Regularly review and revise your policies and practices, obtaining suggestions from parents, other caregivers, health professionals, local public health consultants, and medical authorities. In addition, be sure to have on hand and to consult regularly the most recent editions of definitive documents on health issues in child care. *Healthy Young Children: A Manual for Programs,* available from the National Association for the Education of Young Children (NAEYC), is an excellent and comprehensive guide recommended for all programs. The manual details essential policy information and covers a variety of important health and safety issues. *Caring for Our Children: National Health and Safety Performance Standards: Guidelines for Out-of-Home Child Care Programs* is another indispensable resource, in addition to *Model Child Care Health Policies,* both of which are published

Note: For the health, safety, and well-being of children as well as child care providers, basic health and safety requirements are mandated through legislation, and licensing is usually required for all child care centers and family care homes. In California, for example, the California Department of Social Services, Community Care Licensing, is responsible for this licensing. In addition, the California Department of Education's publication *Visions for Infant/Toddler Care: Guidelines for Professional Caregiving* outlines important health and safety program elements. Check in your state for similar mandates, requirements, and guidelines.

by the American Academy of Pediatrics. The Academy publishes many pamphlets and flyers that are available free of charge or at minimal cost to caregivers and parents.

Guidelines for a Healthy Environment

The following guidelines, which relate directly to caregiving routines, will assist you in preparing appropriate health policies, procedures, and guidelines for your program. (See also the recommendations in the previous section on maintaining a sanitary and safe environment.)

Sanitation

Sanitation is absolutely necessary for keeping children and caregivers healthy. You can maintain a sanitary environment and prevent the spread of germs by following these recommended procedures:

- Adhere strictly to careful handwashing procedures. This is the single most effective means of preventing the spread of illness. Wash your hands frequently throughout the day as you work with children, soaping and rubbing the hand, wrist, and finger areas for at least ten seconds. Use a paper towel to turn off the faucet because faucet handles are loaded with germs. To prevent the spread of germs, wash your hands:

  1. At the start of the day just before working with the children
  2. Before *and* after handling food and feeding children
  3. Before *and* after diapering/toileting a child
  4. Before *and* after your own toileting and personal grooming
  5. After having contact with any bodily fluids (e.g., mucous, saliva, urine), such as when blowing or wiping noses
  6. Before and after any health procedure, such as giving medicine
  7. After cleaning
  8. After handling pets or other animals

  Model for the children appropriate handwashing by showing and telling them when *you* are washing your hands after toileting and before eating. With very young children, it is important to show them how to wash their hands by actually washing their hands and explaining what you are doing. Be sure they wash every time after toileting and diapering and before and after eating.

- Maintain a separate area and sink for food preparation and cleanup. The area for toileting and diapering should be

Model for the children appropriate handwashing by showing and telling them when **you** *are washing your hands after toileting and before eating.*

equipped with its own sink and be situated away from the food preparation area. A separate area and sink should also be available for facility cleanup. Different cleanup cloths should be used in each of the areas and labeled to prevent mix-ups.

- Each day systematically clean and wash all toys by using a dishwasher, washing machine, or bleach solution to sterilize items. Use a solution of one-quarter cup liquid chlorine bleach to one gallon of water. The solution must be prepared daily because it weakens over a day's time and will not be strong enough to kill germs. Put the solution in a clearly marked spray bottle for easy use. (Make sure children are not in the area when you spray the bleach solution and that it is stored out of children's reach.)
- Clean and disinfect all surfaces, including bathrooms, faucet and toilet handles, tables, and floors daily.

Diapering and Toileting

- Use only diaper-changing stations or designated areas for diapering and changing children's soiled clothing. Clean the stations and sanitize with a bleach solution after *each use*. Dispose of cover paper and soiled diapers in a diaper pail or garbage can that is convenient to the caregiver but inaccessible to children. A foot pedal-operated trash can lined with a disposable plastic bag cuts down on germs and should be sanitized regularly. Place the diaper-changing station close enough to a source of warm water so the water can be reached without leaving the child.
- Small, child-sized flush toilets are most appropriate; they are comfortable and sanitary for young children, especially older infants who are just learning to use the toilet. Check that the toilet to be used by the child is clean and has been flushed after previous use.

Feeding and Eating

- Bottles and eating utensils must be washed and sanitized.
- Prepared breast milk, formula, milk, and other perishable foods, including children's lunches brought from home, should be refrigerated at 40 degrees or colder.
- Uneaten food should be discarded if it has been tasted or is perishable.
- Bibs and other "burp" cloths need to be clean and fresh each time they are used.
- Clean feeding/eating tables and sanitize with a bleach solution after each use.

Napping and Resting

- Use separate storage for each child's bedding.
- Wash bedding (sheets, blankets) and wipe the mattress or mat with bleach every week or whenever soiled.
- Parents of children who have contagious illnesses should be called to pick up their child immediately. These children should rest/nap in a separate area from the usual sleeping area while waiting for their parents to arrive.
- Children should sleep with their heads at least three feet apart. To achieve this where space is limited, place cribs, cots, or mats 18 inches apart if children sleep head to foot. More distance between beds creates a less crowded feeling and also facilitates evacuation, if necessary.

Guidelines for Detecting Illness

Caregivers should always be on the lookout for symptoms of illness. A quick check when the child arrives becomes an automatic response. Caregivers must be tuned in to recognize flushed faces, feverish eyes, and changes in breathing. The caregiver's responsibility is to observe the children, report health concerns to parents, and recommend evaluation by a health care provider. Caregivers should not try to diagnose children or prescribe medical treatment.

If the child arrives already ill, it is important to discover that fact before the parent leaves, unless the program has one of those rare facilities set up to take care of sick children. Parents themselves may miss the symptoms because they may lack knowledge about diseases in young children or they may have important reasons not to miss work and thus overlook or dismiss symptoms. The caregiver's job, if that should happen, is not to blame the parent but to be clear about what symptoms are apparent and to explain the policy on sickness. If the child's illness meets exclusion guidelines, the caregiver must refuse to allow the child to stay. If the child's health is in question but he or she does not meet exclusion guidelines, arrangements can be made to keep in touch with the parent during the day.

When children or adults become *seriously ill* during the program, they need individual care and appropriate medical treatment. The common practice is to exclude ill children from a program or ask caregivers not to come to work until they are free from symptoms and are healthy enough to be active again in a group setting.

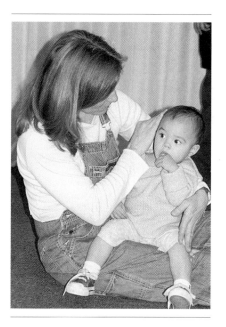

Caregivers should always be on the lookout for symptoms of illness.

95

When a caregiver becomes ill at work, the best policy is to have him or her leave work as soon as possible. In a family child care home, it may be necessary to ask the parents to pick up their children early to allow the provider to take care of himself or herself. Excluding seriously ill adults and children from the program can help to prevent further spread of illness.

Mildly ill children generally do not pose a health threat to the other children or adults in the group. The main issue for caregivers is whether they can realistically care for mildly ill children and the other well children in the group at the same time. Consider the type of illness, the severity of the child's symptoms, how the child is actually feeling, and the caregiver's or program's ability to care for the emotional and physical needs of a mildly ill child.

Whenever a child becomes ill, mildly or seriously, the parent(s) should be notified right away. Infections are most contagious before symptoms appear or when the symptoms first appear and the person starts feeling sick (e.g., shows signs of a sore throat, nausea, diarrhea). In most cases, once the symptoms are obvious, the group has already been exposed to the illness. Different illnesses have different exclusion criteria and waiting periods after treatment has begun. Exclusion policies need to be specific so that parents and staff are clear about when a child is unable to attend.

Sick children must have their emotional needs attended to along with their physical needs. Caring for a mildly or seriously ill child in a group program usually means a balancing act for the caregiver(s). Sick children need a familiar adult to care for them and a quiet place to rest comfortably. This does not have to be in isolation, however, as a sick child may be comforted by being able to watch friends and activities.

When a child becomes ill during the program, assess the severity of the symptom(s). If the symptoms cause discomfort and seem significant, make a careful check for all possible signs of illness.

Recognizing and Responding to Common Symptoms

The following symptoms indicate possible disease or infection in infants and toddlers:

Fever. The child may look flushed or pale and may be warm to the touch. (Your hand on the child's forehead may be deceiving if the hand itself is warm or cold.) When children become ill and show various symptoms, it is important to take their temperature.

The axillary, or armpit, method is best for taking the temperatures of infants and toddlers. *It is neither safe nor practical to use a mouth thermometer with young children.* Use a rectal-type thermometer (with a round, stubby bulb) and place the bulb securely *in the child's armpit*; hold the bulb in place for seven minutes with the child's arm at his or her side. Caregivers should not try to take a child's temperature by placing a thermometer in the child's mouth or rectum.

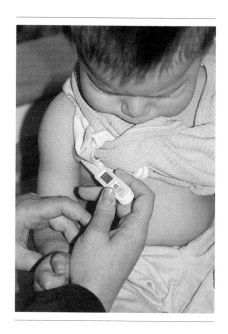

Temperatures taken by the armpit method are one degree lower than those taken orally and two degrees lower than those taken rectally. (*Note:* Fever strips are not reliable indicators of specific temperatures and are not recommended for determining accurate temperatures of young children.)

Unusual behavior. The normally placid child may be more restless than usual. The "ball-of-energy" child may be listless. The usually happy child may be cranky. Crying for no apparent reason may also signal illness. Generally, the child who "is just not herself today" may be exhibiting symptoms of illness.

Changes in skin color or texture. The skin may look red, pale, or yellow. It may have unusual spots or rashes or it may itch.

Changes in the eyes. The whites of the eyes may be red or yellowish and tearing. The lids or the lining of the lids may be red or swollen. There may be discharge.

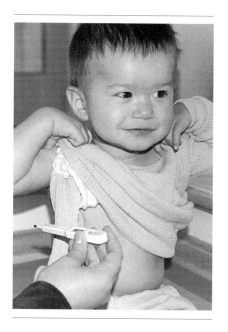

Respiratory difficulties. Problems may range from sniffles and a stuffy nose to coughing and wheezing. There may be either clear or colored discharge from the nose. Look for rapid breathing in the young infant. Changes in breathing rate may be the only indication that something is wrong.

Changes in stools. Diarrhea or loose stools can be either a symptom of another illness or an illness itself. Other changes, such as frequent bowel movements, pale or unusual-colored stools, foul-smelling stools, or blood in stools may be additional symptoms of disease. By keeping track of the consistency and frequency of the child's stools, you will be able to note anything unusual. *Severe diarrhea may result in dehydration, which is extremely dangerous in the very young.*

Changes in urine. Unusually dark, tea-colored urine is a warning sign. Infrequent, scanty urination may signal dehydration.

Changes in appetite. Sick children often do not eat well.

Vomiting. Hard to ignore, vomiting may or may not be a symptom of illness. Some babies spit up frequently; some older infants throw up easily when they cough or gag. Vomiting is a symptom if it is unusual, either in amount or in frequency.

If the child has a fever of 100 degrees or higher by the armpit method (equivalent to 101 or 102 by other methods) and has any symptoms that indicate the child is either infectious or too sick to be in child care, contact the parent(s) to have the child picked up as soon as possible. An infant under four months with an axillary (armpit) temperature of 100 degrees or higher, even without other symptoms, should be excluded.

To contact the parent(s), use the emergency information form the parents filled out when they enrolled the child in the program (see a sample form in Appendix B). The following information needs to appear on the form:

- Current home and work telephone numbers of the parent(s)
- Names, telephone numbers, and relationship of at least two other people who are available to care for the child in case of emergency when the parents cannot be reached immediately
- Name, telephone number, and address of the child's doctor/clinic
- Name of the preferred hospital; insurance information
- Signed permission for emergency treatment

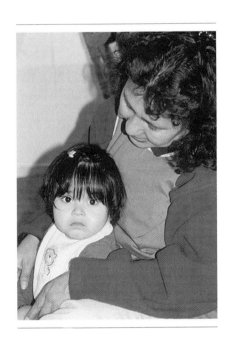

When a child becomes sick or there is an emergency, reaching the parent(s) quickly is very important. Have the parent(s) check the information on the emergency form regularly to be sure the information is accurate. Let all parents know the importance of having correct emergency contact information and ask parents to update the information at least every three to six months or whenever the information changes.

An illness or symptom record should be kept so that information can be clearly communicated to parents and health care providers. These should include signs and symptoms observed, what the caregiver did for the child, who was called, and when.

When a child returns to the program, it is important that he or she feels well enough and has energy to participate fully in the group. Exclusion guidelines indicate when a child can return to the program. In general, if a child's temperature has been 100 degrees (armpit method) or higher, it should be normal for at least 24 hours before the child returns to the program. Programs may also require a release from the child's doctor, especially for illnesses that are highly contagious. (See Appendix D for a copy of a release form to be completed by a physician.)

Child care providers can be an important support to families with children who require temporary or ongoing medications. Caregivers may give authorized medications orally to a child or administer asthma medication with a nebulizer, which allows the child to inhale medication in a mist. However, caregivers are first required to obtain specific training to use a nebulizer and must have documentation that they are personally authorized to do so.

Any prescription medication to be given by the caregiver must be labeled by the pharmacist or the parent with the child's name, the drug's name, and the amount and times to be given. Parents should give written permission for caregivers to administer both prescription and over-the-counter medications (see the sample form in Appendix E).

Check with your health consultant, county public health department, and other medical references, such as the NAEYC publication *Healthy Young Children: A Manual for Programs,* for specific up-to-date treatment and exclusion guidelines for common childhood diseases. Check with licensing and your local health department for information about the availability of training.

Taking Universal Precautions

There is no way to be sure whether any particular child is ill or is carrying a virus or bacteria that could infect other children and adults in the program. Children and adults often carry germs without exhibiting signs of sickness. For this reason, health experts recommend taking universal precautions (i.e., using the same precautions all the time with children and adults regardless of whether they look sick).

Universal precautions begin with careful, consistent hand-washing, as described earlier in this section. Care is required when dealing with children's blood and body fluids because they may be carrying disease-causing pathogens. Always treat blood as a potentially dangerous fluid. Use disposable latex gloves when dealing with a child's cut, bloody nose, oozing skin lesions, or mucous membranes. Remember to remove them with the proper procedure (without touching clean skin to dirty glove), turning them inside out and disposing of them immediately. The video *It's Not Just Routine* (Second edition) includes a demonstration of proper glove use.

Anyone in the program (that is, children, parents, and program staff) who has been exposed to a communicable disease whether severe or not should be notified about the exposure. Caregivers should discuss with parents the importance of notifying the program as soon as possible if the child has been diagnosed with particular communicable diseases. A standard exposure notice should be posted that indicates the date of exposure, the disease, the symptoms to look for, how it is spread, the contagion period, the diagnosis and treatment, and prevention measures. (See Appendix F for a sample exposure notice.) The identity of the child with the disease is kept confidential. Check with your local health department for diseases that should be reported to it and the particular circumstances under which the department's guidelines apply.

Immunization of adults and children is an important and effective means of preventing some infectious diseases or preventing further spread of those diseases among the children and adults in the child care setting. Making sure immunizations are kept up-to-date is a significant part of helping maintain good health in child care programs.

Guidelines for a Safe Environment

As the timeless adage goes, "An ounce of prevention is worth a pound of cure." This saying is certainly applicable to the care of young children. The American Academy of Pediatrics

supervision is needed for the other children and who will call the hurt or ill child's parents. This procedure will allow the primary caregiver to care for the child as long as possible. Family child care providers should have plans to obtain assistance from a nearby neighbor if necessary.

One child's injury or illness will have an impact on the other children in the group. Although you are busy, it is important to be attentive to the rest of the children. They may respond to the situation in various ways. For instance, one child may become distressed, another may seem unfazed, and still another may not notice at all. Do what you can to calm and reassure every child in the group, including the injured child. Explain to the children in simple terms and in a matter-of-fact way what is happening.

As in most other aspects of caregiving, you are being asked again to perform a balancing act. If the emergency is great enough, you will focus, of course, on the injured child. The other children may have to wait for your calm attention until the emergency is over—though some children, because of their own distress, may act out in ways that demand attention during the emergency. While you are busy and distracted with an injured or ill child, other children may incur injuries. Instruct your helping adults to be especially attentive, calm, and reassuring with the children while you attend to the emergency.

Any unusual event in the program affects all the children and adults. Do not simply drop the subject after the emergency is over. Instead, encourage the children who can talk to express their feelings; allow crying as an expression of feelings also. Be as comforting as you can while acknowledging what the children are feeling.

Keeping Records of Injuries

Any time an injury to a child occurs, an injury report must be filled out. A written report provides the parent with a record of the important details so that even minor injuries will not go unnoticed or be forgotten. The person who observed the incident should fill out the report as soon as possible after the injury. In particular, note the date, time, what happened, what action was taken, and by whom (see Appendix G for a sample program log of injuries). An incident report form is provided in Appendix H. Check with state or local licensing agencies in your area to see whether there are requirements for reporting children's injuries.

Notifying Parents

Whenever a child has an injury that requires medical attention beyond minor first aid for a scrape or small bump, notify the parents right away. Parents should also be notified immediately of any injuries to the head or falls, which may have caused internal injuries, even when the child seems to recover quickly.

Guidelines for Emergency Drill Procedures

Monthly drills to ensure emergency preparedness may be required by state or local licensing agencies. Even if there are no requirements for regular drills, caregivers are responsible for developing a detailed procedure for fire and earthquake and other disasters. The procedures should be part of the orientation of all new staff members and parents. In addition, both the parents and the staff need to make disaster plans for their own families, and that information needs to be discussed and incorporated, when feasible, into the child care program's plan. For example, in case of an earthquake, which parent will try to reach the child in child care? How will staff members cope with the needs of the child care program and those of their own children?

Periodically during the year the procedures should be reviewed with all staff and in group parent and staff meetings. Check with local agencies for emergency drill procedures for different types of disasters that may occur in your area.

The same person should schedule and conduct a fire drill once a month.

Listed below are some basic guidelines for fire and earthquake drill procedures.

Fire Drills

The same person should schedule and conduct a fire drill once a month. The drills should take place at different times of the day to practice evacuation during activities at different locations. When the alarm sounds, immediately evacuate all the children: carry infants or place them in a crib and push them to the holding area away from the building; walk or carry older infants to the holding area. Take attendance to account for all children and adults before anyone returns to the building. Document the time necessary to evacuate the building for each drill. All caregivers should critique the procedure for future improvement.

In case of a real fire, anyone on the premises who notices the fire should sound the alarm and call the local fire department (remember this emergency phone number is to be posted by each telephone). For some buildings it is possible for the alarm to register at the local fire department. Evacuate children to the holding areas and keep them there until the building is cleared by the fire department. Take attendance to account for all children and adults before anyone returns to the building. If necessary, notify parents to come and pick up their children. In any event, parents should be informed about the fire and its possible impact on the children.

Earthquake Drills

Earthquake drills also need to be conducted on a regular basis. Older children who can understand should be taught to "duck and cover" in the room they are in, crawling under tables and away from windows and other glass. Practice this procedure every month in a matter-of-fact way with the children, both inside and out-of-doors. During the practice drills, explain *in very simple terms* that if there were an earthquake the floor or ground would shake. To be safe from falling debris, everyone must "duck and cover," getting under the tables when inside the building or to an open space out-of-doors. The open space outside should be away from power lines or poles, trees, glass, high structures that might fall, and the like.

When infants are indoors, gather them together away from mirrors, windows, and other glass. Large pillows can be used to corral the children. If possible, gather the infants in a spot that

When making disaster plans, be sure the plans are safe and practical to use with the children.

offers protection from falling debris. If outdoors, gather the infants around you in an open space, away from power lines or poles, trees, glass, high structures that might fall, and so on.

When making disaster plans, be sure the plans are safe and practical to use with the children. Any adults who are part of the program but not directly responsible for children must know they are essential during a disaster and will be needed to assist with all the children and adults in the entire program. The assignment of those adults should be part of the disaster preparedness plan. Arranging for the availability of parents and extra helping adults should be a part of the plan. In case of a gas leak, directions for finding the gas main and and turning it off to prevent fire should also be part of the plan.

Emergency kits equipped with flashlights, batteries, and other emergency supplies, including a cache of food and water for at least three days, additional first aid supplies, blankets, extra clothing and diapers, adult and child medications, and spare eyeglasses should be stored in an area or areas most likely to be accessible and undamaged in the event of a real earthquake.

If a real earthquake occurs, children and adults should take cover wherever they are at the time of the quake. If children are inside, they should remain inside, but they should be moved outside as soon as it is safe to do so. Keep the children in the outside holding area until you determine it is safe to return to the building. Take attendance to account for all children and adults before anyone returns to the building. The disaster plan should include arrangements for notifying parents when it is necessary to come and pick up their children. Arrangements should also include plans to care for the children until the parents are able to pick them up.

Points to Consider

1. Do you have clearly written health and safety policies and guidelines for your program? Do you give copies of the policies and guidelines to your parents when they enroll their child(ren) in your program and do you go over the guidelines during the parent orientation to your program?
2. Do you have up-to-date emergency information adjacent to your telephone and signed releases for all of the children as well as emergency telephone numbers of paramedics, the fire department, the police department, poison control center, and available helping adults?

3. Do you know how to maintain a safe and healthy environment and how to prevent illnesses and injuries whenever possible?

4. Have you child-proofed your environment from the child's viewpoint (get down on your hands and knees to get the real perspective) for safety and health while still providing an enriched environment that says "yes" to the child to explore and be curious?

5. Do you and the other caregivers know how to respond to various symptoms of illness and how to give first aid in case of injury? Do you have a completely stocked first aid kit and emergency supplies on hand in case of emergency?

6. Do you have plans or ideas about how to maintain a calm social–emotional climate during times of illness and injury?

Suggested Resources

Books and Articles

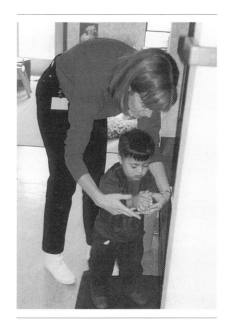

American Academy of Pediatrics, Committee on Infectious Diseases. *2000 Red Book Report of the Committee on Infectious Diseases* (24th edition). Elk Grove Village, Ill.: American Academy of Pediatrics, 2000.

The first new edition in three years advances the *Red Book*'s mission for the twenty-first century with the most current information on clinical manifestations, etiology, epidemiology, diagnosis, and treatment of more than 200 childhood infectious diseases. It was developed with the assistance and advice of hundreds of physician contributors from across the country. The new edition contains many significant revisions, updates, and additions to its authoritative content.

Caring for Our Children: National Health and Safety Performance Standards: Guidelines for Out-of-Home Child Care Programs. Prepared by American Public Health Association staff and American Academy of Pediatrics staff. Elk Grove Village, Ill.: American Academy of Pediatrics, 2000.

Contains guidelines on the health and safety needs of children from birth to twelve years in family and group child care homes and centers. It includes information on licensing, the child-to-staff ratio, emergency procedures, prevention and control of injury and infectious diseases, special needs, and so forth. Also contains information from the Consumer Product Safety Commission about crib safety.

Green, Martin I. *A Sigh of Relief: First-Aid Handbook for Childhood Emergencies* (Revised edition). New York: Bantam Books, 1984.

Contains fast, simple instructions for handling childhood injuries and illnesses.

Handal, Kathleen A. *American Red Cross First Aid and Safety Handbook.* Boston: Little, Brown & Company, 1992.

This comprehensive guide to administering first aid in emergency situations is based on course materials used by Red Cross chapters across the country. The step-by-step instructions are accompanied by 175 line drawings.

Healthy Young Children: A Manual for Programs. Edited by A. S. Kendrick, R. Kaufman, and K. P. Messenger. Washington, D.C.: National Association for the Education of Young Children, 1995.

Available from the National Association for the Education of Young Children, 1834 Connecticut Ave., NW, Washington, DC 20009-5786. This basic manual is used in early childhood programs to promote the health and safety of children, staff, and families. Designed for ease in finding information, it is frequently used as a textbook.

Keeping Kids Healthy: Preventing and Managing Communicable Disease in Child Care. Sacramento: California Department of Education, 1995.

This manual is designed for use in child care settings with children from birth to five years. It contains chapters on understanding, preventing, recognizing, and managing communicable disease. A list of resources is included.

Model Child Care Health Policies (Third edition). Prepared by the Pennsylvania Chapter of the American Academy of Pediatrics. Elk Grove Village, Ill.: American Academy of Pediatrics, 1997.

Contains model health policies that can be adapted or used selectively in any type of child care setting. The policies are designed to allow caregivers to insert information specific to their sites. This publication also contains reproducible forms and resource lists.

Moukaddem, V. "Preventing Infectious Diseases in Your Child Care Setting," *Young Children,* Vol. 45 (1990), 28–29.

Presents information about infectious diseases and how to control them in a child care environment.

Nash, M., and C. Tate. "Health, Safety and First Aid," in *Better Baby Care: A Book for Family Day Care Providers.* Washington, D.C.: The Children's Foundation, 1986, pp. 87–103.

Offers sound advice and suggestions on how to handle health and safety concerns with infants and toddlers in family child care. Also useful for center-based caregivers.

Setting Up for Infant/Toddler Care: Guidelines for Centers and Family Child Care Homes (Revised edition). Edited by Annabelle Godwin and Lorraine Schrag. Washington, D.C.: National Association for the Education of Young Children, 1996.

Includes practical information regarding business aspects of setting up a child care program. Experts describe how to promote all areas of a child's development.

Smith, Lendon. *The Encyclopedia of Baby and Child Care* (Revised edition). Englewood Cliffs, N.J.: Prentice Hall, 1981.

Contains information about emergencies, first aid, poisonings, fevers, and allergies—as well as what you need to know about the anatomy and development of infants and toddlers.

Willis, Anne, and Henry Ricciuti. *A Good Beginning for Babies: Guidelines for Group Care.* Washington, D.C.: National Association for the Education of Young Children, 1975.

Contains a chapter on health and safety as well as a list of symptoms and a sample letter for parents regarding illness.

Audiovisuals

Caring for Our Children. Elk Grove Village, Ill.: National Association for the Education of Young Children, 1995. Six 30-minute videocassettes.

The six videos show how to comply with the health and safety guidelines set forth in the manual of the same title. Each video clearly presents the appropriate steps to take to ensure safe and healthy out-of-home care.

It's Not Just Routine: Feeding, Diapering, and Napping Infants and Toddlers (Second edition). Sacramento: California Department of Education (with WestEd), 2000. Videocassette, color, 24 minutes; printed guide.

Updated version of the video illustrates health and safety concerns in the caregiving routines of feeding, diapering, and napping, including the use of protective gloves and universal precautions. Emphasizes the role of routines in building the relationship between infants and caregivers and in infant learning.

Space to Grow: Creating a Child Care Environment for Infants and Toddlers. Sacramento: California Department of Education (with WestEd), 1988. Videocassette, color, 22 minutes; printed guide.

Presents eight concepts, including health and safety, to consider in setting up environments for infants and toddlers.

Web Sites

California Department of Social Services *<http://www.dss.cahwnet.gov>*

Centers for Disease Control *<http://www.cdc.gov>*

American Academy of Pediatrics *<http://www.aap.org>*

Information Hotline

California Child Care Health Line: 1-800-333-3212
This hotline provides child care health and safety information Monday through Thursday, 8 a.m. to 4 p.m.

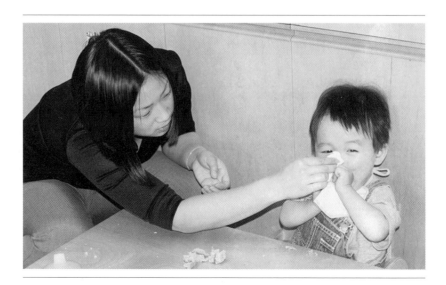

Section Eight: Recordkeeping

Caregivers must keep records. This section deals with records that pertain directly to individual children and their families and concentrates on those that make up a developmental profile. Daily records of the various caregiving activities have been discussed in other sections and will not be repeated here, but those records may also be part of the developmental profile.

One purpose of keeping records is to build a picture of each child's development so that caregivers can plan individualized programs. The picture includes the child's range of general and specific needs at the present time and the family's expectations. By looking at the individual picture, caregivers can plan a program to respond to each participant.

The Importance of Written Records

Sometimes caregivers believe they do not have to keep written records of individual development, but recordkeeping is

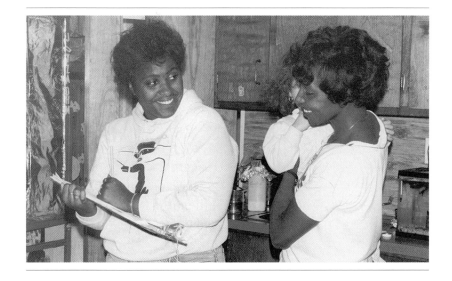

One purpose of keeping records is to build a picture of each child's development so that caregivers can plan individualized programs.

critical to quality care. Records are used to plan for individualizing the curriculum for each child. They also help the caregiver identify developmental concerns and work with parents and specialists to get evaluation and intervention if needed. Experienced caregivers assess the children's development informally every day because they know each child, what he or she can do, and what he or she cannot do. Even beginning caregivers usually can see growth and development in children quite easily, but written records are still important. Often caregivers' memories play tricks on them. Without written records patterns are harder to detect.

Sometimes, patterns of developmental lags become evident, and the child may need more than the carefully planned individualized program can provide. Caregivers may notice lags without formal training in developmental assessment. They can compare individual developmental checklists that they have completed (see a sample developmental checklist in Appendix I) with standardized developmental charts.

A word of caution—be very careful about comparing one child to another or using the chart to determine anything but pronounced developmental lags. Do not use the chart as a basis for writing report cards. Each child's development is individual. There is a wide range of typical development. If you begin to label children "advanced" or "average" or "slow" at this tender age, you do them and their parents a grave disservice. Labeling a child becomes a *self-fulfilling prophecy* in which expectations influence the outcome. Do not let a label influence a child's future. Developmental profiles do not predict future success or

Each child's development is individual. No child is average.

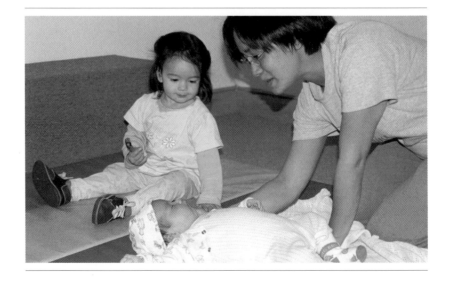

failure in either school specifically or life in general. The exception is at either extreme of the scale. If the child's development is extreme, you will notice it without needing a developmental chart.

Sources of Information

There are three ways to gather information: through observations, forms, and interviews. Caregivers' careful observations of children provide valuable information that cannot be obtained any other way. Caregivers should develop careful observation skills and should consider the time spent observing as important as anything else they do. Observing and recording situations and behaviors help caregivers get to know each child as an individual, understand what he or she needs at any given time, assess development, and plan for next steps.

Besides the information gained from observing, the following information should be gathered:

1. Developmental history, including at what age the child reached major milestones (rolled over, started to walk), and individual information, such as words for bodily functions, fears, favorite toys, and the like. (See Appendix J for a sample form.)

2. Health history, including special prenatal and birth circumstances, chronic health conditions, food allergies, medication needed, and so forth.

3. Nutrition information, such as type of formula, introduction of solid foods, and food preferences. (See Appendix C for a sample form.)

4. Child-rearing practices, including types of guidance and family expectations for the child.

5. Family background, including family makeup, family members, ages of siblings, language spoken in the home, cultural values, parental preferences regarding care of the child, and so forth.

6. Special considerations, such as social services requests and the like.

Sample forms provided in the appendixes indicate how some of the information can be organized. For example:

• "Infant Diet/Meal Plan." The form (see Appendix C) ensures that parents and caregivers share the same knowledge about which solid foods already have been introduced, the type of formula used, whether the baby is breast-fed, and the schedule for introducing new foods.

- "Medication Release." The form (see Appendix E) gives caregivers permission to administer medication needed by the child while he or she is in child care.
- "Physician's Report Form—Day Care Centers." A pre-admission health evaluation (see Appendix D) by a physician is a licensing requirement and provides an expert opinion on the child's health and health history. Sometimes a medical condition can give clues to developmental patterns. For example, a baby with a history of ear infections needs to be watched for signs of temporary hearing loss, which may result in delayed language development.
- "Developmental Health History." A preadmission health history (see Appendix J) reported by the parent is also helpful in evaluating development.

The sample form adapted from NAEYC's publication *Healthy Young Children* is fairly simple and general, but it goes beyond a simple health history and records information on daily routines, habits, the parent's evaluation of the child's personality, and special considerations—likes and dislikes, fears, and so on.

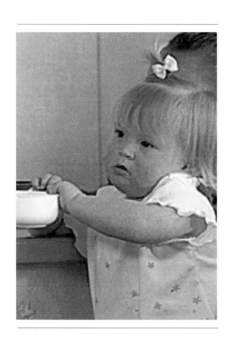

In addition to the forms, caregivers' notes based on knowledge of and interviews with the family round out the file. Information may come from informal daily contacts but should also come from planned, formal parent conferences held at regular intervals. The child's growth and development should be the focus of the conferences.

Each child's file should contain specific up-to-date information on the child's development in each of the following areas:

1. Social–emotional development
2. Physical development
3. Language development
4. Cognitive development

The sample checklist included in Appendix I is the Desired Results Developmental Profile for infants and toddlers currently being developed by the California Department of Education, Child Development Division. It can be used regularly to assess each child's development. By keeping such records, you can chart specific progress in various developmental areas.

Be sure that all records remain confidential. This sort of information is not to be passed around. Records should be in locked file cabinets, not available to other parents or visitors.

Points to Consider

1. How well do the records you keep provide a developmental profile of each child in your care? In what ways can you improve your recordkeeping?

2. In what ways do you use the developmental profile you have of each child (either in your head or on paper) to make daily, weekly, monthly plans? (Consider the ways in which you set up the environment, plan for materials and activities, plan approaches to dealing with behaviors, make changes in caregiving routines.)

3. In what ways do you plan for the enhancement of the social–emotional, physical, language, and cognitive development of each child in your care?

Suggested Resources

Books and Articles

American Academy of Pediatrics, Committee on Infectious Diseases. *2000 Red Book Report of the Committee on Infectious Diseases* (24th edition). Elk Grove Village, Ill.: American Academy of Pediatrics, 2000.

The first new edition in three years advances the *Red Book*'s mission for the twenty-first century with the most current information on clinical manifestations, etiology, epidemiology, diagnosis, and treatment of more than 200 childhood infectious diseases. It was developed with the assistance and advice of hundreds of physician contributors from across the country. The new edition contains many significant revisions, updates, and additions to its authoritative content.

Beaty, Janice J. *Observing Development of the Preschool Child.* Columbus, Ohio: Merrill Publishing Co., 1986.

Presents a system of observing the child two to six years of age and recording emotional, social, motor, cognitive, language, and creative development.

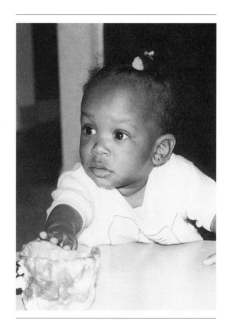

Caring for Our Children: National Health and Safety Performance Standards: Guidelines for Out-of-Home Child Care Programs. Prepared by American Public Health Association staff and American Academy of Pediatrics staff. Elk Grove Village, Ill.: American Academy of Pediatrics, 2000.

Contains guidelines on the health and safety needs of children from birth to twelve years in family and group child care homes and centers. It includes information on licensing, the child-to-staff ratio, emergency procedures, prevention and control of injury and infectious diseases, special needs, and so forth. Also contains information from the Consumer Product Safety Commission about crib safety.

Cohen, Dorothy H., and Virginia Stern. *Observing and Recording the Behavior of Young Children* (Third, revised edition). New York: Columbia University, Teachers College, Teachers College Press, 1983.

Focuses mostly on preschool age but includes a chapter on observing infants and toddlers.

Developmentally Appropriate Practice in Early Childhood Programs Serving Children from Birth to Age 8. Edited by Sue Bredekamp. Washington, D.C.: National Association for the Education of Young Children, 1986.

Part Two contains guidelines and information on how infants and toddlers develop.

The First Twelve Months of Life. Edited by Frank Caplan. New York: Bantam Books, 1984.

Describes growth and development month by month and contains 12 growth charts as well as several photographs.

Keeping Kids Healthy: Preventing and Managing Communicable Disease in Child Care. Sacramento: California Department of Education, 1995.

This manual is designed for use in child care settings with children from birth to five years. It contains chapters on understanding, preventing, recognizing, and managing communicable disease. A list of resources is included.

The Second Twelve Months of Life. Edited by Frank Caplan. New York: Bantam Books, 1982.

Describes growth and development during the second year of life.

Setting Up for Infant/Toddler Care: Guidelines for Centers and Family Child Care Homes (Revised edition). Edited by Annabelle Godwin and Lorraine Schrag. Washington, D.C.: National Association for the Education of Young Children, 1996.

Includes practical information regarding business aspects of setting up a child care program. Experts describe how to promote all areas of a child's development.

Audiovisuals

Caring for Our Children. Elk Grove Village, Ill.: National Association for the Education of Young Children, 1995. Six 30-minute videotapes.

The six videos show how to comply with the health and safety guidelines set forth in the manual of the same title. Each video clearly presents the appropriate steps to take to ensure safe and healthy out-of-home care.

Section Nine:
Special Issues with Children and Families

amilies are the biggest and most important influence in a child's life. Caregivers support children best by being in alliance with families; understanding their cultural roots, their individual differences, and the challenges they may face; and helping to support parents. In the United States there are families from many different countries of origin, representing a wide variety of religious, ethnic, language, and cultural backgrounds. Child-rearing patterns and parenting styles vary both within and across the different groups. That is as it should be. Variety is a healthy and positive social reality.

There are, however, cases in which a child or a family is clearly defined as needing extra support. These cases include families in which:

- Children are neglected or abused.
- Parents have been or are involved in substance abuse.
- Children have chronic illness or physical disabilities.

Any family may be affected. Special situations like those named above are not restricted to any particular group or social class. The children in these families, like all children, need consistency, safety, appropriate sensory experiences, and attachment. When children come to child care with a history of challenging needs, the caregiver should understand what those needs are and how to meet them. Responding to children's unmet needs is more important than diagnosing the condition.

Child Abuse and Neglect

Young children, unfortunately, are sometimes targets of abuse and neglect by adults responsible for their care. These adults may include the parents, relatives, babysitters, child care providers, or any other adults who come into contact with the child. Abuse may occur in many forms, including physical, emotional, verbal, and sexual abuse.

Physical abuse includes hitting, shaking, and burning children and other forms of physical punishment, such as tying a child to a chair or bed, closing or locking children in a closet, and so forth. Failing to provide a child with adequate food or other necessities, such as clothing, failing to change the child's diapers or clothing regularly, or leaving the child wet or soiled for long periods of time is also abusive, though it may be classified as neglect rather than abuse. Such maltreatment can cause serious illness or create unhealthy conditions.

Suspicious Injuries and Unusual Behaviors

As a caregiver you may notice bruises, burns, or other injuries on children in your care that seem slightly (or highly) suspicious. Injuries that are recurrent or unexplained or do not make sense for the child's particular age are all signs of possible abuse. Those injuries are not the ordinary scraped knees of beginning walkers or the bumps of new crawlers. Injuries that indicate possible abuse oftentimes appear in places that are not usually bumped or banged, such as on the child's back or abdomen or around the genitals.

If parents' explanations of a particular injury are strange or inconsistent, you may well have cause for concern. Suspicious injuries or unusual behaviors may indicate child abuse. Sometimes the injuries are coupled with unusual behavior on the part of the child. Some abused children are especially withdrawn; others act out a great deal and exhibit very difficult behavior. Some children may be overly tuned-in to adults and adults' feelings and may seem wary of adults; such children are anxious, scared, or even cautiously trying to please every adult in sight.

Sexually abused children oftentimes act out adult sexual behaviors that generally are unknown to young children unless they have learned them from older children or adults. Other specific physical signs of sexual abuse may include difficulty sitting or walking because of pain, itching, or bruises around the rectal or genital area; bloody or stained undergarments; regressive soiling or wetting the pants or bed. Behavioral signs are similar to those listed above for other types of abuse.

The Caregiver's Legal Obligation

Child abuse is obviously a serious matter. It is important to protect a child from abusive adults. Your legal obligation as a caregiver is quite clear: *you must report suspected child abuse.* You do not have to prove you are right; all you have to do is suspect abuse. When you suspect abuse, you are legally obliged to call either the police or the local Child Protective Services (CPS) agency and report your suspicions. The agency will ask you to file a written report (also a legal obligation) within 36 hours and then the agency will follow up with an investigation in cases it deems necessary.

For further guidelines to help you decide when something is suspicious enough for you to report, see the *Child Abuse Prevention Handbook,* published by the Office of the Attorney General in Sacramento. Another helpful resource is *Making a Difference,* a handbook and videotape training package for child care providers published by the California Child Care Resource and Referral Network in San Francisco.

A full understanding of the complexities of child abuse and neglect is important for everyone who works in child care. The topic should be included periodically in preservice and in-service training for both child care providers and parents.

Some children may arrive in your care unwashed, unfed, unchanged—and you may suspect their condition is the result of parental neglect. It is important to determine whether the child is truly neglected or whether the parents' perception of good care simply differs from yours. The care may be adequate but different from what you would provide. For example, differences in care may stem from differences in cultural values and beliefs. However, if the child is truly suffering from parental neglect, it must be reported for the good of the child.

The Abused Child's Need for Trust

The task of the infant during the first year is to establish trust. Usually trust develops naturally as attachment grows, needs are met promptly, and the infant comes to see the world as a friendly, safe place. Abused infants and toddlers may have difficulty forming a sense of basic trust if they lack attachment, if they are battered, or if they are neglected. Although you have little control over the lives of abused children when they are not in your care, you can concentrate on doing your best to meet their needs when they are in your care.

Suspicious injuries and unusual behaviors may indicate child abuse.

If you suspect child abuse, you should report it.

The following tips help young or mobile infants to develop trust:

1. Provide a consistent, predictable environment.

2. Respond quickly to any indication that the child needs something. Do not make him or her wait too long to be fed or changed.

3. Help the child establish an attachment in the program by assigning one person, a primary caregiver, to care for the child. If the child is in care longer than the working hours of one caregiver, then a second caregiver should be assigned to the child. This approach provides children the consistency of having one person in the child care program they can count on to "attach to" and trust rather than the unpredictability of never knowing who will care for them. By consistently being the person to feed and diaper, the primary caregiver will come to know each child's unique temperament, behavioral characteristics, and personality. The caregiver, like the infant, will form an attachment—each one to the other.

4. Support parents rather than blame them. It is important but hard to do when you are dealing with an infant in distress. Parents batter or neglect because they are not able to get their own needs met. Parents, too, need help and support.

5. Consult the authorities and experts available to you for support and for advice on how to handle the child, the parents, and the situations that may arise.

Older infants also may be dealing with trust issues. You can help older infants by following the guidelines for young infants. In addition, you may need to be especially understanding about difficult behavior. Older infants who do not trust may have difficulty at naptime, for instance. They may feel vulnerable when going to sleep; therefore, they will fight against sleeping. Or perhaps the difficult behavior centers on eating. Older infants may be particularly crabby at mealtimes. So while you are guiding and controlling the difficult behavior, think about what may be causing it.

Attachment remains a primary issue for older infants. Although your caregiver–child ratio may be larger for the over-two age group, it is still very important to help each older infant attach to one caregiver. As trust develops in infants, so trust grows in older infants when they can depend on one particular person to provide for their primary care. In other words the primary caregiving system that fosters attachment helps the older infant establish and maintain trust.

The Abused Older Infant's Need for Autonomy

Abused or neglected older infants may be stunted in their movement toward self-control and independence. *Infant/Toddler Caregiving: A Guide to Social–Emotional Growth and Socialization* gives further information about the need for autonomy as well as how to respond to it.

You can help the abused or neglected older infant who is deficient in the area of self-control and independence by doing the following:

1. Patiently and gently teach control and provide control for the older infant when necessary. Abused older infants may be extra aggressive with other children. You have to be firm about stopping the aggression (such as hitting, biting, hair pulling) but be gentle and understanding at the same time.
2. Give attention to the withdrawn child and help him or her become more outgoing. Encourage social interactions with other children. Encourage the child to explore the environment by providing interesting, age-appropriate toys and activities. Provide extra support for the withdrawn older infant in order to draw the child out of his or her shyness and insecurity.
3. Encourage the child's expression of his or her feelings. The abused or neglected child may be angry or fearful or perhaps both. Because words are limited in older infants, actions may be the only way those feelings can be expressed. Help the older infant to use words to express feelings and describe needs and wants while you guide the child so that his or her

Abused infants and toddlers may not develop a sense of basic trust if they lack attachment, if they are battered, or if they are neglected.

actions do not harm anyone or anything. Particular materials and activities in the program can be especially helpful. For example, water play, playdough, pounding boards, and dramatic play are time-honored play activities that provide a means for children to express their feelings by a soothing activity, vigorous physical play, or acting out of experiences and feelings.

4. Help parents to understand appropriate developmental expectations and to develop means of coping with and controlling difficult behavior in effective, nonabusive ways. If you can establish and maintain a positive and supportive relationship with the parent(s), you may be able to make a significant contribution to the life of the child as well as the family.

Caregivers' Reactions

Be aware of your own feelings about the abused child. Caregivers may find it difficult to like some children. These children may trigger anger in all the adults around them. Be aware of your feelings and the child's behaviors that are connected to those feelings. If you feel aggressive toward the child, put extra energy into responding in firm but *gently* controlling ways. The child may expect adults to act aggressively, to cause pain. The child's behavior may trigger urges in you to do just that. Resist those urges. Abused children have an extra need for *gentle* rather than tough control. If your negative feelings persist, seek professional support for yourself so you can confront and deal with your own feelings as well as meet the critical emotional needs of the abused child. Also become aware of your feelings toward the family. See the child as part of the family and do not take sides. Blaming parents or families makes it hard to support them, and that is what they most need.

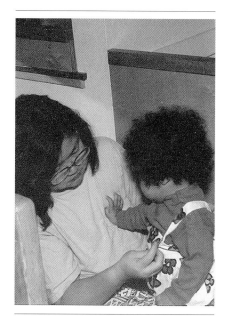

Be aware of your own feelings about the abused child. Caregivers may find it difficult to like some children.

Substance Abuse

Babies of alcohol- and drug-addicted mothers or of mothers who used alcohol or drugs while they were pregnant are often in child care programs. Large numbers of newborn infants each year have been exposed to potentially health-threatening drugs in utero.

Physical and Behavioral Characteristics

Babies born of mothers who used drugs or alcohol may have had many challenges to their development by the time they get to you. The behaviors exhibited by babies exposed prenatally to abusing substances as well as their physical conditions are complicated by a number of factors, such as prenatal history, prematurity, and low birth weight. The babies may also have undergone withdrawal at the beginning of their lives.

The problems those babies face may include difficulty in sleeping, extreme hypersensitivity, and irritability. They may cry a great deal and have outbursts of screaming. They may be especially tense, restless, hypertonic, and generally overexcitable. Jittery movements, hyperactivity, and shutting out stimulation are other common behaviors. Or the babies may be excessively sleepy and not very responsive even when awake. They may have increased muscle tone and be "rigid," or they may be the opposite—have decreased muscle tone and be "floppy." If the parent was an intravenous drug user before or during pregnancy or both, the baby may be born with hepatitis or human immuno-deficiency virus (HIV), which can lead to AIDS. Those diseases, passed from mother to baby, are contracted from using contaminated needles.

The babies may also have been born with cognitive and developmental disabilities, cerebral palsy, or other physical conditions, such as facial, cardiac, genital, or urinary abnormalities. These babies are also especially susceptible to stroke and sudden infant death syndrome (SIDS).

The babies' physical and behavioral problems related to parental substance abuse may be complicated by additional problems of the lifestyle at home. Frequently, parents who abuse substances have poor nutrition and so do their infants. Parents may neglect self-care as well as baby care. An unstable home life with lack of consistency may be present as well. Attachment may be shaky. Parents who are substance abusers may lack basic child care information. In short, little about the parent's life may be conducive to healthy and nurturing child rearing.

If you, the caregiver, have neither knowledge of nor experience with the special behaviors and physical needs of babies affected by substance abuse, you may well wonder what to do when such a baby enters your care. Meeting children's needs can be a fulfilling activity, but the needs of babies born of substance abusers are difficult to meet. For instance, when you put the babies down to sleep, they do not sleep but cry and fuss instead. When they finally go to sleep, they wake up again before they are fully rested. The babies are sometimes so irritable that they

The babies may also have been born with cognitive and developmental disabilities, cerebral palsy, or other physical conditions, such as facial, cardiac, genital, or urinary abnormalities. These babies are also especially susceptible to stroke and sudden infant death syndrome (SIDS).

124

are hard to care for and be around. Their crying and outbursts of screaming are hard on the other children in your care, too. The infants' tenseness and restlessness give the message that you cannot make them comfortable, no matter what you do.

The hardest part about relating to the babies affected by substance abuse is that the caregiving routines you use effectively with other children often do not consistently bring the same rewards and satisfactions to you or the affected infants. Of course, some caregivers find rewards in responding to the challenges that such babies present. Working with babies who are so needy can be deeply satisfying when you find you can make a difference in their young lives.

Usually, difficult babies will "grow out of it," but oftentimes the infants affected by substance abuse continue to have difficulties as they get older. The behaviors they exhibited as young infants may well continue and become magnified as life gets more complicated and more is required of them. For example, common behaviors may include continued irritability, easy frustration, distractibility, aggressive and impulsive behavior, hyperactivity, temper tantrums, insecure attachments, cognitive and language difficulties, and the inability to become toilet trained. Those behaviors may be a result of prenatal exposure to drugs or alcohol or a result of their stressful home life. Commonly the behaviors result from a combination of factors. In any case such behaviors make caring for a young child very difficult.

Caring for Hard-to-Comfort Infants and Toddlers

What can you do? You must do what you can to meet the child's needs even though neither of you ever seems satisfied. You must continue to look for ways to comfort the hard-to-comfort child. For instance, a young infant who is hypersensitive may benefit from reduced stimulation by being in a quiet, darkened environment or by being swaddled—that is, being wrapped tightly in a receiving blanket with only the face exposed. A mobile infant may be comforted by being held firmly and lovingly. Slow and gentle touches, singing, and soft words can help children of any age.

When the child is older and is able to move around and interact with other children, you must look for effective ways to guide behavior. You must firmly and lovingly set clear limits and guidelines for the child as well as control unacceptable behavior. Children in your care who exhibit behaviors indicative of severe

The hardest part about relating to the babies affected by substance abuse is that the caregiving routines you use effectively with other children often do not consistently bring the same rewards and satisfactions to you or the affected infants.

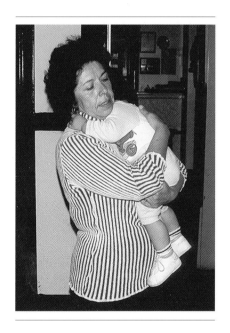

A young infant who was exposed to cocaine may be helped by being swaddled.

emotional problems make caregiving very difficult or impossible in a group setting, especially if the behavior is seriously threatening to the child, the child's peers, or the adults in the program. *Infant/Toddler Caregiving: A Guide to Social–Emotional Growth and Socialization* will help you understand and guide in healthy and effective ways the behavior of children who have serious difficulties. In addition, parent education and support are necessary.

Of course, you cannot do the job alone—you may need to get support services for the child and the parent. Check your community resources for agencies and professionals who work therapeutically with children and families.

While you are getting support services for the child and family, do not forget yourself. Do not try to cope alone. Find help. Discuss your concerns with other staff members, your supervisors, and other caregivers. Pick up the phone book and find out which local agencies can help you.

Chronic Illnesses and Physical Disabilities

Children with a variety of special conditions can be and should be accommodated in group child care settings. Usually the best approach is to determine the appropriateness for both the individual child/family and the program on a case-by-case basis. For example, you might care for a child with chronic asthma or an infant with a cleft palate who still needs additional surgeries. The child with asthma would require special monitoring for breathing difficulties and possibly medication during an

Children with a variety of special conditions can be and should be accommodated in group child care settings.

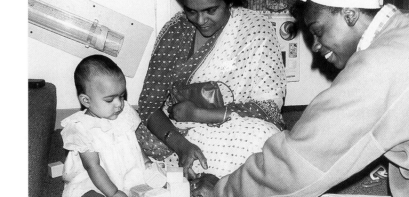

attack. The child with a cleft palate would need special care in feeding until the surgical repairs had been completed. Other examples of special conditions include a child with seizures who would need regular medication and special supervision and a child recovering from a serious illness who might need a period of convalescence and require a special schedule with restricted activities. Each circumstance will have its own unique issues and special care needs. Parents and the health professionals working with the child and family can advise you of the special care required.

Only some of the needs of children with special conditions are different from the needs of the typically developing child; many needs are the same. All children need attention, relationships, protection, food, toileting or changing, sleep, and sensory experiences. However, young infants with chronic diseases, medical problems, or disabling conditions may need more time to learn to trust those who care for them.

If infants have been in and out of the hospital, had numerous caregivers, and experienced painful medical procedures, their sense of trust may be weakened. The child care program needs to provide consistent care by a primary caregiver in a predictable environment in order to help the child regain or develop trust. Primary caregiving means that one person (or possibly two when the child's day is longer than the caregiver's working hours) greets and cares for the child throughout the day during all caregiving routines—providing consistent care for the infant day after day, week after week. The intention of the primary caregiving system is to provide consistent care for the infant by one adult, or at most two adults, throughout the day and throughout the child's enrollment in the particular child care program.

Mobile and older infants may also have trust issues to resolve. In addition, they need opportunities for exploration and interaction with materials, objects, and peers. Perhaps some children have been protected or restricted from exploration and interaction beyond what was necessary. While they are exploring and interacting, older infants will run into situations where they need consistent limits. Some people find it hard to be firm with children who have chronic illnesses or disabilities. Nevertheless, special treatment beyond what the children's medical or physical conditions warrant is a disservice to those children and the others in the group.

Only some of the needs of children with special conditions are different from the needs of the typically developing child; many needs are the same. All children need attention, relationships, protection, food, toileting or changing, sleep, and sensory experiences.

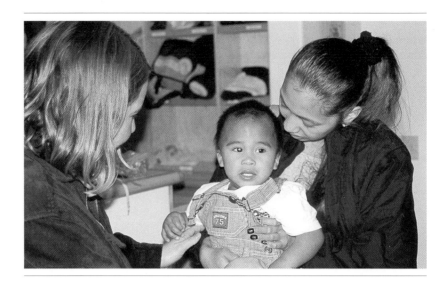

Find out exactly what each child needs for his or her special circumstances. Perhaps the child needs to be held in certain positions to be comfortable. Or feeding may need to be done in a certain way. The child may have a special diet. Perhaps the child has little energy for exertion and may be easily overstressed; therefore, you have to restrict his or her activity level. The child may need some specialized treatment or therapy that you will have to administer. Perhaps some particular exercises are important for the child's development.

Some children with chronic illnesses or with particular medical conditions may have an underactive immune system. Those children need more protection from ordinary germs than do other children. It is important that you educate all caregiving staff and all of the parents in the program so they fully understand the special issues of concern for the children and do not regard legitimate health concerns as arbitrary or overprotective.

Communication with parents is vital if you are to meet a child's special needs.

Communication with parents is vital if you are to meet a child's special needs. Let the child's parent(s) know how important it is to alert you to any warning signs that may signal problems for the child. A health history form is important for recording information, including medications or treatments to be administered, instructions on how to carry out caregiving routines in ways that meet the child's special needs, monitoring requirements, behavioral characteristics related to the condition, possible side effects of medications, and what constitutes an emergency as well as instructions about how to handle it.

Points to Consider

1. Are you able to look at all children under your care as children first and children with conditions, histories, or problems second? If not, do you have some ideas about how to change that situation?

2. Do you have some ideas about how to keep the atmosphere as caring and pleasant as possible even when the behaviors of a particular child work against that?

3. Do you know how to determine what each child in your program needs?

4. How much do you know about changing behaviors? Do you have some ideas about how to increase your knowledge?

5. How much do you know about the outside resources available to you, to the children in your program, and to their families?

Suggested Resources

Books and Articles

American Academy of Pediatrics, Committee on Infectious Diseases. *2000 Red Book Report of the Committee on Infectious Diseases* (24th edition). Elk Grove Village, Ill.: American Academy of Pediatrics, 2000.

The first new edition in three years advances the *Red Book*'s mission for the twenty-first century with the most current information on clinical manifestations, etiology, epidemiology, diagnosis, and treatment of more than 200 childhood infectious diseases. It was developed with the assistance and advice of hundreds of physician contributors from across the country. The new edition contains many significant revisions, updates, and additions to its authoritative content.

Caring for Our Children: National Health and Safety Performance Standards: Guidelines for Out-of-Home Child Care Programs. Prepared by American Public Health Association staff and American Academy of Pediatrics staff. Elk Grove Village, Ill.: American Academy of Pediatrics, 2000.

Contains guidelines on the health and safety needs of children from birth to twelve years in family and group child care homes and centers. It includes information on licensing, the child-to-staff ratio, emergency procedures, prevention and control of injury and infectious diseases, special needs, and so forth. Also contains information from the Consumer Product Safety Commission about crib safety.

Child Abuse Prevention Handbook. Sacramento: Office of the Attorney General, 1985.

Provides an overview of the laws, practices, and procedures for preventing, detecting, reporting, and treating child abuse.

Fauvre, M. "Including Young Children with 'New' Chronic Illnesses in an Early Childhood Education Setting," *Young Children*, Vol. 43 (1988), 71–78.

Discusses how teachers can respond to children with chronic disease or medical conditions. Gives practical information about older children that can be applied easily to infants and toddlers and guidelines for assessing the quality of programs for infants and toddlers.

Healthy Young Children: A Manual for Programs. Edited by A. S. Kendrick, R. Kaufman, and K. P. Messenger. Washington, D.C.: National Association for the Education of Young Children, 1995.

This basic manual is used in early childhood programs to promote the health and safety of children, staff, and families. Designed for ease in finding information, it is frequently used as a textbook.

Infant/Toddler Caregiving: A Guide to Social–Emotional Growth and Socialization. Sacramento: California Department of Education, 1990.

Presents information on temperaments and offers suggestions for caregiving.

Keeping Kids Healthy: Preventing and Managing Communicable Disease in Child Care. Sacramento: California Department of Education, 1995.

This manual is designed for use in child care settings with children from birth to five years. It contains chapters on understanding, preventing, recognizing, and managing communicable disease. A list of resources is included.

Lewis, Keeta. *Infants and Children with Prenatal Alcohol and Drug Exposures: A Guide to Identification and Intervention.* North Branch, Minn.: Sunrise River Press, 1995.

Provides an understanding and general knowledge about the effects prenatal substance abuse has on the growth and development of infants and children.

Making a Difference. San Francisco: California Child Care Resource and Referral Network, 1986.

Created specifically for caregivers. Provides information on preventing and reporting child abuse and neglect.

Setting Up for Infant/Toddler Care: Guidelines for Centers and Family Child Care Homes (Revised edition). Edited by Annabelle Godwin and Lorraine Schrag. Washington, D.C.: National Association for the Education of Young Children, 1996.

Includes practical information regarding business aspects of setting up a child care program. Experts describe how to promote all areas of a child's development.

Audiovisuals

Caring for Our Children. Elk Grove Village, Ill.: National Association for the Education of Young Children, 1995. Six 30-minute videotapes.

The six videos show how to comply with the health and safety guidelines set forth in the manual of the same title. Each video clearly presents the appropriate steps to take to ensure safe and healthy out-of-home care.

Getting in Tune: Creating Nurturing Relationships with Infants and Toddlers. Sacramento: California Department of Education (with WestEd), 1988. Videocassette, color, 24 minutes; printed guide.

Presents the "responsive process," which includes three steps: watching, asking, and adapting. Helps the caregiver learn what a young child needs and how best to respond to that need.

Human Development: A New Look at the Infant—Attachment (Program 5). Irvine, Calif.: Concept Media, 1983. Videocassette or filmstrip/sound cassette, color, 27 minutes; printed guide.

Reviews Mary Ainsworth's work in the area of attachment. Discusses attachment behaviors and the role they play in separations and reunions. Explores the importance of caregiver sensitivity. Available from Concept Media, P.O. Box 19542, Irvine, CA 92713-9542.

Respectfully Yours: Magda Gerber's Approach to Professional Infant/Toddler Care. Sacramento: California Department of Education (with WestEd), 1988. Videocassette, color, 55 minutes; printed guide.

Presents Magda Gerber's philosophy based on respecting the baby.

Room at the Table: Meeting Children's Special Needs at Mealtime. Sacramento: California Department of Education (with WestEd), 1996.

All children are capable of growing, learning, and responding to love no matter what their abilities as long as they have caring adults who believe in them. This video has valuable information on ways to include children with special needs in child care programs and to adapt mealtime to those needs. The second half shows caregivers and experts demonstrating exciting techniques for meeting children's individual needs.

Appendixes

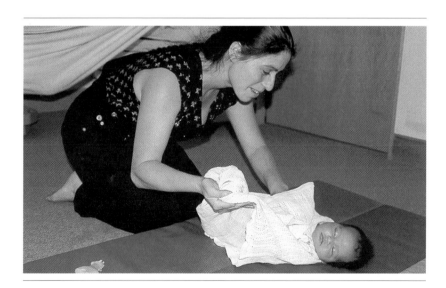

Appendix A

Information Sheet

Date ________________________

Baby's Name

Feedings

Sleep

Diapers or Toileting Information

Other

Comments

Appendix B

Identification and Emergency Information

STATE OF CALIFORNIA
HEALTH AND HUMAN SERVICES AGENCY

CALIFORNIA DEPARTMENT OF SOCIAL SERVICES
COMMUNITY CARE LICENSING DIVISION

IDENTIFICATION AND EMERGENCY INFORMATION

CHILD CARE CENTERS

To Be Completed by Parent or Guardian

CHILD'S NAME LAST	MIDDLE	FIRST	SEX	TELEPHONE ( )
ADDRESS NUMBER STREET	CITY	STATE ZIP		BIRTHDATE
FATHER'S NAME LAST	MIDDLE	FIRST		BUSINESS TELEPHONE ( )
HOME ADDRESS NUMBER STREET	CITY	STATE ZIP		HOME TELEPHONE ( )
MOTHER'S NAME LAST	MIDDLE	FIRST		BUSINESS TELEPHONE ( )
HOME ADDRESS NUMBER STREET	CITY	STATE ZIP		HOME TELEPHONE ( )
PERSON RESPONSIBLE FOR CHILD LAST NAME MIDDLE FIRST		HOME TELEPHONE ( )		BUSINESS TELEPHONE ( )

ADDITIONAL PERSONS WHO MAY BE CALLED IN AN EMERGENCY

NAME	ADDRESS	TELEPHONE	RELATIONSHIP

PHYSICIAN OR DENTIST TO BE CALLED IN AN EMERGENCY

PHYSICIAN	ADDRESS	MEDICAL PLAN AND NUMBER	TELEPHONE ( )
DENTIST	ADDRESS	MEDICAL PLAN AND NUMBER	TELEPHONE ( )

IF PHYSICIAN CANNOT BE REACHED, WHAT ACTION SHOULD BE TAKEN?

☐ CALL EMERGENCY HOSPITAL ☐ OTHER EXPLAIN: _____

NAMES OF PERSONS AUTHORIZED TO TAKE CHILD FROM THE FACILITY
(CHILD WILL NOT BE ALLOWED TO LEAVE WITH ANY OTHER PERSON WITHOUT WRITTEN AUTHORIZATION FROM PARENT OR GUARDIAN)

NAME	RELATIONSHIP

TIME CHILD WILL BE CALLED FOR

SIGNATURE OF PARENT OR GUARDIAN	DATE

TO BE COMPLETED BY FACILITY DIRECTOR/ADMINISTRATOR

DATE OF ADMISSION	DATE LEFT

LIC 700 (5/99)(CONFIDENTIAL)

Infant Diet/Meal Plan

Child's name _____ Birth date ___ / ___ / ___

           (Last)   (First)

Foods already introduced:

Type of formula _____

Is your child breast-fed? ☐ Yes   ☐ No

Schedule for introducing new foods:

        Baby's Age   *Food*

_____   _____

Parent's signature   Caregiver's signature

Appendix D

Physician's Report Form—Day Care Centers

STATE OF CALIFORNIA—HEALTH AND HUMAN SERVICES AGENCY   DEPARTMENT OF SOCIAL SERVICES—COMMUNITY CARE LICENSING

PHYSICIAN'S REPORT—CHILD CARE CENTERS
(CHILD'S PRE-ADMISSION HEALTH EVALUATION)

PART A – PARENT'S CONSENT (TO BE COMPLETED BY PARENT)

_____, born _____ is being studied for readiness to enter
(NAME OF CHILD)   (BIRTH DATE)

_____ . This Child Care Center/School provides a program which extends from ____ : ____
(NAME OF CHILD CARE CENTER/SCHOOL)

a.m./p.m. to _____ a.m./p.m. , _____ days a week.

Please provide a report on above-named child using the form below. I hereby authorize release of medical information contained in this report to the above-named Child Care Center.

_____   _____
(SIGNATURE OF PARENT, GUARDIAN, OR CHILD'S AUTHORIZED REPRESENTATIVE)   (TODAY'S DATE)

PART B – PHYSICIAN'S REPORT (TO BE COMPLETED BY PHYSICIAN)

Problems of which you should be aware:

Hearing: Allergies: medicine:

Vision: insect stings:

Developmental: food:

Language/Speech: asthma:

                                                            other:

Other (Include behavioral concerns):

Comments/Explanations:

MEDICATION PRESCRIBED/SPECIAL ROUTINES/RESTRICTIONS FOR THIS CHILD:

IMMUNIZATION HISTORY: (Fill out or enclose California Immunization Record, PM-298.)

VACCINE	DATE EACH DOSE WAS GIVEN				
	1st	2nd	3rd	4th	5th
POLIO (OPV OR IPV)	/ /	/ /	/ /	/ /	/ /
DTP/DTaP/ DT/Td (DIPHTHERIA, TETANUS AND [ACELLULAR] PERTUSSIS OR TETANUS AND DIPHTHERIA ONLY)	/ /	/ /	/ /	/ /	/ /
MMR (MEASLES, MUMPS, AND RUBELLA)	/ /	/ /			
HIB MENINGITIS (REQUIRED FOR CHILD CARE ONLY) (HAEMOPHILUS B)	/ /	/ /	/ /	/ /	
HEPATITIS B	/ /	/ /	/ /		
VARICELLA (NOT REQUIRED) (CHICKENPOX)	/ /	/ /			

SCREENING OF TB RISK FACTORS (listing on reverse side)

☐ Risk factors not present; TB skin test not required.

☐ Risk factors present; Mantoux TB skin test performed (unless previous positive skin test documented).

____ Communicable TB disease not present.

I have ☐   have not ☐   reviewed the above information with the parent/guardian.

Physician: _____   Date of Physical Exam: _____
Address: _____   Date This Form Completed: _____
Telephone: _____   Signature _____

☐ Physician   ☐ Physician's Assistant   ☐ Nurse Practitioner

LIC 701 (6/99) (Confidential)

137

Appendix E
Medication Release

Date _____

Parent's Instructions—Children receiving medication at a child care facility must have:

1. Original prescription bottle with the name of the medication, the date, the child's name, the prescribing physician's name, dosage, and times to be given clearly indicated.
2. Written consent from the parent permitting child care facility personnel to give medication to the child and specifying the times per day to be given.

Any medication to be given to the child for longer than two weeks must be accompanied by the physician's written instructions and signature in addition to the parent's signature.

Name of child _____

Name of medication _____

Dosage _____ Times to be given_____

I hereby authorize the child care personnel to assist in the administration of medications

described above from_____ until _____
                            (Date)   (Date)

_____   _____
      (Parent's signature)   (Date)

- -

Physician's Release (Required for any medication given for longer than a two-week period.)

Diagnosis _____

Name of medication and dosage _____

Times to be given per day _____

Length of time to be given _____

_____   _____
      (Physician's signature)   (Date)

Appendix F
Sample Exposure Notice

Note: The information contained below does not replace consultation with your physician if your child is sick.

Dear Parents:

On (date) _____ your child may have been exposed to the following disease:

_____

Onset of disease after exposure (how long): _____

The symptoms: _____

This disease is spread by: _____

It is contagious (when, for how long, at what stage): _____

It can be recognized/diagnosed by: _____

Steps for treatment: _____

Steps for prevention: _____

Note to staff: See Appendix A of *Keeping Kids Healthy* for important facts about 26 communicable diseases most frequently encountered in child care programs.

Appendix G
Program Log of Injuries

Date	Time	Child's Name	Location	Accident	Action Taken	Initials

Appendix H

Incident Report Form

Fill in all blanks and boxes that apply.

Name of program: _____ Phone: _____

Address of facility: _____

Child's name: _____ Sex: M __ F __ Birth Date:__/__/__ Incident Date:__/__/__

Time of incident: am/pm   Witnesses: _____

Parent(s) notified by: _____ Time Notified: am/pm

Location where incident occurred: ☐ playground ☐ classroom ☐ bathroom ☐ hall ☐ kitchen ☐ doorway
☐ large muscle room or gym ☐ office ☐ dining room ☐ stairway ☐ unknown
☐ other (specify) _____

Equipment/product involved: ☐ climber ☐ slide ☐ swing ☐ playground surface ☐ sandbox ☐ trike/bike
☐ hand toy (specify):_____
☐ other equipment (specify): _____

Cause of injury (describe): _____
☐ fall to surface: estimated height of fall _____ feet: type of surface: _____
☐ fall from running or tripping ☐ bitten by child ☐ motor vehicle ☐ hit or pushed by child
☐ injured by object ☐ eating or choking ☐ insect sting/bite ☐ animal bite
☐ injury from exposure to cold ☐ other (specify): _____

Parts of body injured: ☐ eye ☐ ear ☐ nose ☐ mouth ☐ tooth ☐ other face ☐ other part of head ☐ neck
☐ arm/wrist/hand ☐ leg/ankle/foot ☐ trunk ☐ other (specify):_____

Type of injury: ☐ cut ☐ bruise or swelling ☐ puncture ☐ scrape ☐ broken bone or dislocation ☐ sprain
☐ crushing injury ☐ burn ☐ loss of consciousness ☐ unknown ☐ other (specify): _____
_____

First aid administered at the facility (e.g., pressure, elevation, cold pack, washing, bandage): _____
_____

Treatment provided by: _____
☐ No doctor's or dentist's treatment required
☐ Treatment as an outpatient (e.g., office or emergency room)
☐ Hospitalized (overnight) # of days: _____

Number of days of limited activity from this incident: _____ Follow-up plan for care of the child: _____
_____

Corrective action needed to prevent reoccurrence: _____

Name of official/agency notified: _____ Date: _____

Signature of staff member: _____ Date: _____

Signature of parent: _____ Date: _____

copies: 1) child's folder, 2) parent, 3) injury log

Used with permission of the American Academy of Pediatrics; adapted from *Model
Child Care Health Policies,* Early Childhood Education Linkage System (ECELS), 1997.

Appendix I

Desired Results Developmental Profile

(Draft version)

Birth Through Seven Months

	Met	*Emerging*	*Not Met*

Child Desired Result 1:
Children are personally and socially competent.

Indicator 1:
Children show self-awareness and a positive self-concept.

1. Explores own body (e.g., observes hands, clasps hands together, explores one hand with the other) _____ _____ _____

Indicator 2:
Children demonstrate effective social and interpersonal skills.

2. Signals caregiver for assistance (e.g., cries, grunts, yells; smiles, gestures, or moves to initiate social contact) _____ _____ _____

3. Maintains eye contact with person looking at him or her (e.g., stares back at person looking or trying or engage him or her, mutually gazes with others) _____ _____ _____

4. Shows preference for interacting with familiar people (e.g., watches or listens for return of familiar people, can usually be comforted by familiar adult, nestles into the arms of a familiar adult) _____ _____ _____

5. Shows interest in other children (e.g., looks at or turns toward other babies; touches peers' hair, face, or other body part) _____ _____ _____

Indicator 3:
Children demonstrate effective self-regulation of their behavior.

6. Comforts self by clutching, sucking, or stroking when tired or stressed (e.g., calms while stroking or holding soft blanket or toy) _____ _____ _____

7. Looks intently, gestures, smiles, and/or makes sounds to start, maintain, or stop social contact (e.g., squirms, looks away or cries when uncomfortable; pushes unwanted items away) _____ _____ _____

8. Anticipates being lifted or fed and moves body to participate (e.g., quiets body when picked up, shapes body to fit adult) _____ _____ _____

9. Signals when full (e.g., turns head away, pushes with tongue or hand) _____ _____ _____

Indicator 4:
Children show awareness, acceptance, understanding, and appreciation of others' special needs, gender, family structures, ethnicities, cultures, and languages.

Indicator 5:
Children show growing abilities in communication and language.

10. Reacts to human voice (e.g., turns toward conversations, quiets self, appears to watch or listen)   _____   _____   _____

11. Distinguishes familiar voices from other sounds (e.g., turns toward familiar voices)   _____   _____   _____

12. Makes a variety of repetitive sounds or gestures (e.g., babbles, coos, or uses hand shapes to express self)   _____   _____   _____

13. Expresses several clearly differentiated cries (e.g., anger, hunger)   _____   _____   _____

14. Uses gestures or signals to indicate needs or feelings (e.g., kicks feet, waves arms; expresses pleasure and eagerness with sounds or laughter)   _____   _____   _____

15. Imitates sounds or gestures made by caregiver (e.g., responds "ba" to caregiver saying "ba," smiles in response to caregiver's smile)   _____   _____   _____

Child Desired Result 2:
Children are effective learners.

Indicator 1:
Children are interested in learning new things.

16. Directs attention toward caregiver's face or voice (e.g., focuses on caregiver's face, reaches for face/voice)   _____   _____   _____

17. Directs attention toward objects by reaching, grasping, or staring at them _____   _____   _____

18. Reacts to new objects, voices, sounds, etc., by becoming more quiet or active   _____   _____   _____

Indicator 2:
Children show cognitive competence and problem-solving skills through play and daily activities.

19. Looks for or orients toward dropped object   _____   _____   _____

20. Uses more than one sense at one time (e.g., uses sight, touch, and hearing by examining and shaking a toy for the sound; mouthing and banging a toy)   _____   _____   _____

21. Acts on an object to make a pleasing sight, sound, or motion continue (e.g., kicks or swats mobile, continues to bat at object to repeat sound)   _____   _____   _____

Indicator 3:
Children show interest in real-life mathematical concepts.

22. Creates own patterns of self-regulation for sleeping, eating, and wakeful play   _____   _____   _____

Indicator 4:
Children demonstrate emerging literacy skills.

23. Explores books (e.g., fingers or looks at books and pictures)   _____   _____   _____

Child Desired Result 3:
Children show physical and motor competence.

Indicator 1:
Children demonstrate an increased proficiency in motor skills.

24. Lifts head _____ _____ _____

25. Holds head up _____ _____ _____

26. Rolls over _____ _____ _____

27. Inches forward or backward on stomach or back _____ _____ _____

28. Claps hands _____ _____ _____

29. Pounds on things with hands _____ _____ _____

30. Kicks at objects _____ _____ _____

31. Holds arms out for jacket or lifts arms so T-shirt can be taken off _____ _____ _____

32. Brings object to mouth _____ _____ _____

33. Grasps, releases, regrasps, and releases object again _____ _____ _____

34. Exhibits some eye-hand coordination (e.g., transfers and manipulates objects with hands) _____ _____ _____

35. Follows a slowly moving object with eyes _____ _____ _____

Eight Months Through Seventeen Months

Child Desired Result 1:
Children are personally and socially competent.
Indicator 1:
Children show self-awareness and a positive self-concept.

1. Responds with gestures or vocal signals when name is spoken   _____ _____ _____

2. Identifies familiar objects (e.g., body parts; when prompted, finds clothes, blanket, or toy by pointing or reaching)   _____ _____ _____

3. Shows preferences (e.g., plays with one toy more than others; reaches, points, or moves toward desired objects or people)   _____ _____ _____

4. Shows appropriate emotions (e.g., smiles, waves, or claps hands when successful at completing an activity; shows frustration at interruption or inability to do something him/herself)   _____ _____ _____

Indicator 2:
Children demonstrate effective social and interpersonal skills.

5. Looks to adult for messages about appropriate and inappropriate behavior, frequently checking for caregiver's presence in unfamiliar situations (e.g., brings toys from toy box back to caregiver, follows caregiver around)   _____ _____ _____

6. Distinguishes between familiar and unfamiliar adults (e.g., is at ease around familiar adults, shows pleasure or relief at approach of primary caregiver or parent, shows preference to be comforted by familiar adult)   _____ _____ _____

7. Uses physical gestures or sounds to get help from familiar adults (e.g., tugs on caregiver; moves, points, or motions to objects out of reach)   _____ _____ _____

8. Shows preference among play partners (e.g., recognizes and shows affection for familiar peer by hugging, running toward, or leaning against peer)   _____ _____ _____

9. Plays side-by-side with another child using same or similar toys (e.g., plays nearby other child or children using trucks, dolls, or sand at the same time)   _____ _____ _____

10. Participates in spontaneous interactions with peers (e.g., makes faces, imitates silly actions or sounds)   _____ _____ _____

Indicator 3:
Children demonstrate effective self-regulation of their behavior.

11. Comforts self by retrieving familiar objects or engaging in routines (e.g., holds comfort blanket or toy; sings or babbles self to sleep)   _____ _____ _____

12. Expresses own needs, such as being hungry or wanting an object of comfort   _____ _____ _____

13. Anticipates and participates in routine activities (e.g., lifts arms toward caregiver to be picked up; cooperates in dressing)   _____ _____ _____

Met   Emerging   Not Met

Indicator 4:
Children show awareness, acceptance, understanding, and appreciation
of others' special needs, gender, family
structures, ethnicities, cultures, and languages.

Indicator 5:
Children show growing abilities in communication and language.

14. Turns to look at object when named (e.g., ball, person)   _____   _____   _____

15. Understands simple one-step requests (e.g., when feeding, "Please open your mouth"; when playing, "Can you get the ball?")   _____   _____   _____

16. Expresses two or three understandable words (e.g., "ba" for bottle, "mama," "dada," "no," "bye-bye")   _____   _____   _____

17. Expresses self using gestures, movements, intonation, or facial expression (e.g., shakes head "no," nods "yes"; uses personalized gesture, smiles, frowns, points)   _____   _____   _____

18. Takes turns in back-and-forth sound play with caregiver that mimics a conversation (e.g., responds to caregiver's speech by producing words or by babbling sounds in reply as if taking turns in a conversation)   _____   _____   _____

Child Desired Result 2:
Children are effective learners.

Indicator 1:
Children are interested in learning new things.

19. Manipulates things in the environment (e.g., moves toward, bangs, fingers, touches, and mouths objects)   _____   _____   _____

20. Investigates new phenomena (e.g., reaches out to touch rain, stops play to watch shadow move)   _____   _____   _____

Indicator 2:
Children show cognitive competence and problem-solving skills
through play and daily activities.

21. Remembers location of favorite objects (e.g., asks for objects out of sight, persists in search for a desired object when it is hidden)   _____   _____   _____

22. Shows basic awareness of cause and immediate effects (e.g., opens and closes, presses key or button to make noise)   _____   _____   _____

23. Uses another object or person as a tool (e.g., asks to be picked up to reach something, uses block to get ball from tight space, pulls string to bring toy within hand reach)   _____   _____   _____

Indicator 3:
Children show interest in real-life mathematical concepts.

24. Understands "more" in reference to food or play (e.g., uses "more" or responds appropriately when asked if he/she wants more crackers, more music, more swinging)   _____   _____   _____

146

25. Uses simple nesting or stacking toys (e.g., nests three to four cups, stacks three to four blocks of graduated size)   _____   _____   _____

26. Understands time words such as "after," "before" (e.g., "After we change your diaper, we will read a story," "Before we go outside, we have to put on our coats.")   _____   _____   _____

27. Explores spatial relationships (e.g., attempts to fit own body in boxes or tunnels, fingers holes in a pegboard, fills and dumps bucket with toys)   _____   _____   _____

28. Groups a few objects by shape, color, or size (e.g., finds two or three toys that have the same simple shape, color, or size)   _____   _____   _____

Indicator 4:
Children demonstrate emerging literacy skills.

29. Points or makes sounds when looking at picture books   _____   _____   _____

30. Enjoys touching, carrying, and looking at books   _____   _____   _____

31. Brings book to caregiver   _____   _____   _____

32. Shows pleasure when read to (e.g., vocalizes, smiles, sustains interest)   _____   _____   _____

33. Grasps marker or crayon and makes marks on paper   _____   _____   _____

Child Desired Result 3:
Children show physical and motor competence.

Indicator 1:
Children demonstrate an increased proficiency in motor skills.

34. Sits up   _____   _____   _____

35. Crawls or creeps on hands and knees   _____   _____   _____

36. Pulls to stand   _____   _____   _____

37. Stands and cruises while holding onto furniture   _____   _____   _____

38. Walks alone   _____   _____   _____

39. Runs   _____   _____   _____

40. Stops and walks backwards a few steps   _____   _____   _____

41. Climbs simple structures (e.g., slides, playground structures)   _____   _____   _____

42. Throws objects   _____   _____   _____

43. Carries objects   _____   _____   _____

44. Pushes objects   _____   _____   _____

45. Pulls objects   _____   _____   _____

46. Scoots on or rides wheel toys without pedals   _____   _____   _____

47. Dumps objects from container   _____   _____   _____

48. Releases objects into container   _____   _____   _____

49. Scoops and rakes with hand to manipulate or pick up objects, sand, food, etc.   _____   _____   _____

	Met	Emerging	Not Met
50. Uses thumb and forefinger to pick up small items	_____	_____	_____
51. Feeds self (e.g., handles cup with minimal spilling, handles spoon for self-feeding)	_____	_____	_____

Child Desired Result 4:
Children are safe and healthy.

Indicator 1:
Children show an emerging awareness and
practice of safe and healthy behavior.

	Met	Emerging	Not Met
52. Washes and dries hands with caregiver assistance	_____	_____	_____
53. Can be distracted from unsafe behavior with verbal limits, physical prompt, or signal from caregiver (e.g., avoids object if told it is hot, can be redirected from activity if caregiver warns about potential danger)	_____	_____	_____

Eighteen Through Thirty-Five Months

Child Desired Result 1:
Children are personally and socially competent.

Indicator 1:
Children show self-awareness and a positive self-concept.

1. Recognizes self in mirror or photographs (e.g., points to or says own name to select his or her photo from among two or more photographs)   _____   _____   _____

2. Uses names of self and others (e.g., "Me Joel," signed or spoken)   _____   _____   _____

3. Shows awareness of being seen by others (e.g., exaggerates or repeats behavior when he/she notices someone is watching)   _____   _____   _____

4. Acts as though he/she is capable of doing anything (e.g., sweeps the floor with an adult-sized broom; "I get it," "Me do it myself.")   _____   _____   _____

Indicator 2:
Children demonstrate effective social and interpersonal skills.

5. Periodically checks back with caregiver for help or reassurance when playing independently or with peers (e.g., calls or looks across room for caregiver)   _____   _____   _____

6. Uses words or actions to request assistance from familiar adults (e.g., asks familiar adults for help to get toys or resolve conflicts with peers)   _____   _____   _____

7. With adult direction, finds items needed for an activity (e.g., uses adult's suggestions to find missing pieces to a toy or items needed for an art activity)   _____   _____   _____

8. Approaches or seeks out a particular peer to be near or play with   _____   _____   _____

9. Engages in joint exploration and some peer play (e.g., plays with others in sandbox, joins in spontaneous small-group games such as *Ring Around the Rosie* or *Hokey Pokey*)   _____   _____   _____

10. Shows concern for a child who is crying or in distress (e.g., stops playing after noticing that another child is hurt)   _____   _____   _____

11. Creates role play, modeling everyday activities (i.e., being a mommy, daddy, or baby; vacuuming, sweeping, cooking, talking on phone)   _____   _____   _____

Indicator 3:
Children demonstrate effective self-regulation of their behavior.

12. Exhibits the beginnings of impulse control and self-regulation (e.g., says "No" when reaching for forbidden object, restrains self from stepping on a book on the floor)   _____   _____   _____

13. Anticipates and follows multistep, daily routines when prompted (e.g., washes hands and helps set table at snack time, helps to pick up and put away blocks at clean-up time)   _____   _____   _____

Indicator 4:
Children show awareness, acceptance, understanding, and appreciation of others' special needs, gender, family structures, ethnicities, cultures, and languages.

14. Notices differences (e.g., pats others' hair, stares at someone who is different) _____ _____ _____

Indicator 5:
Children show growing abilities in communication and language.

15. Understands a variety of simple two-step requests (e.g., "Pick up the book and bring it here.") _____ _____ _____

16. Understands names for common objects, familiar people, actions, and expressions (e.g., identifies or points to people, objects, clothing items, toys, or actions when they are named) _____ _____ _____

17. Learns and uses new vocabulary in everyday experiences _____ _____ _____

18. Combines words into simple sentences (e.g., "Go potty," "I want to play," "Keisha have car") _____ _____ _____

19. Asks and answers simple questions (e.g., "Go to park now," "Where is mommy?") _____ _____ _____

Child Desired Result 2:
Children are effective learners.

Indicator 1:
Children are interested in learning new things.

20. Independently explores the immediate environment to investigate what is there (e.g., asks about a new toy he/she finds, actively searches through collection of toy cars) _____ _____ _____

21. Tries new activities, materials, and equipment (e.g., shows willingness to try unfamiliar art materials, musical instruments, toys) _____ _____ _____

Indicator 2:
Children show cognitive competence and problem-solving skills through play and daily activities.

22. Uses familiar objects in combination (e.g., spoon in bowl, doll in bed, person in car) _____ _____ _____

23. Acts out simple dramatic play themes with others (e.g., "You baby, me mommy," pretends to be an animal) _____ _____ _____

24. Works simple "insert" puzzles (e.g., completes three-piece simple puzzle, uses simple shape sorter box) _____ _____ _____

Indicator 3:
Children show interest in real-life mathematical concepts.

25. Counts to two or three (e.g., recites, "one, two, three") _____ _____ _____

26. Imitates counting rhymes or songs (e.g., "Three Little Monkeys"; "One, Two, Buckle My Shoe") _____ _____ _____

27. Uses some number words (e.g., asks for "two," says there are "three" ants) _____ _____ _____

28. Fills and empties containers (e.g., with sand or water) _____ _____ _____

29. Shows interest in patterns or sequence (e.g., attempts to use or follow patterns with materials such as peg boards, magnetic shapes, stringing beads) _____ _____ _____

30. Shows some understanding of daily time sequence (e.g., time to eat, time to go home, group time, nap time) _____ _____ _____

31. Matches simple shapes in form boards and puzzles (e.g., circles, squares, triangles) _____ _____ _____

32. Classifies, labels, and sorts objects by group (e.g., hard vs. soft, large vs. small, heavy vs. light; by colors) _____ _____ _____

33. Arranges objects in lines (e.g., makes a row of blocks) _____ _____ _____

Indicator 4:
Children demonstrate emerging literacy skills.

34. Names objects or actions in pictures or books _____ _____ _____

35. Recognizes signs and symbols in the environment (e.g., identifies stop sign, identifies label or logo from boxes of favorite cereal) _____ _____ _____

36. Memorizes phrases of songs, books, and rhymes _____ _____ _____

37. Looks through picture books, magazines, catalogs as if he/she is reading (e.g., turns several pages, makes sounds that relate to pictures in book, turns pages at right time) _____ _____ _____

38. Scribbles with marker or crayon _____ _____ _____

39. Names scribbles (tells others about what scribbles are) _____ _____ _____

Child Desired Result 3:
Children show physical and motor competence.

Indicator 1:
Children demonstrate an increased proficiency in motor skills.

40. Stands and walks on tip toes _____ _____ _____

41. Walks backwards _____ _____ _____

42. Walks up stairs holding a hand or railing _____ _____ _____

43. Catches a ball by trapping it with arms and hands _____ _____ _____

44. Pounds object with intent and precision (e.g., hammers peg with accuracy) _____ _____ _____

45. Creates simple block structures _____ _____ _____

46. Pushes foot into shoe _____ _____ _____

47. Takes off shoes _____ _____ _____

48. Rides tricycle using pedals most of the time _____ _____ _____

49. Uses a paintbrush _____ _____ _____

	Met	*Emerging*	*Not Met*
50. Holds object with one hand and manipulates it with the other (e.g., winds music box while holding it, spins blades of toy helicopter, brushes doll's hair)	_____	_____	_____
51. Folds blanket, cloth diaper, or papers	_____	_____	_____
52. Pours liquid from small pitcher or cup	_____	_____	_____

Child Desired Result 4:
Children are safe and healthy.

Indicator 1:
Children show an emerging awareness and practice of safe and healthy behavior.

	Met	*Emerging*	*Not Met*
53. Washes and dries hands without assistance	_____	_____	_____
54. Uses tissue to wipe nose with help	_____	_____	_____
55. Tries some new foods	_____	_____	_____
56. Pays attention to safety instructions (e.g., cooperates when told, "I need to hold your hand while we cross the street.")	_____	_____	_____

Developmental Health History

Child's name _____ Birth date _____ / _____ / _____
               (Last)   (First)

Nickname _____

Physical health

What health problems has your child had in the past? _____

_____

What health problems does your child have now? _____

_____

_____

Other than what you listed above, does your child have any allergies? If so, to what? _____

_____

_____

How severe? _____

Does your child take any medicine regularly? If so, what? _____

_____

Has your child ever been hospitalized? If so, when and why? _____

_____

Does your child have any recurring chronic illness or health problem (such as asthma or

frequent earaches)? _____

_____

Does your child have a disability that has been diagnosed (such as cerebral palsy, seizure

disorder, developmental delay)? _____

_____

Do you have any other concerns about your child's health?_____

_____

_____

Adapted from *Healthy Young Children* (National Association for the Education of Young Children, 1995).

Development (compared with other children this age)

Does your child have any problems with talking or making sounds? Please explain. _____

_____

Does your child have any problems with walking, running, or moving? Please explain. _____

_____

Does your child have any problems seeing? Please explain. _____

_____

Does your child have any problems hearing? Please explain. _____

_____

Does your child have any problems using her or his hands (such as with puzzles, drawing, small

building pieces)? Please explain. _____

_____

Daily living

What is your child's typical eating pattern? _____

_____

_____

Write N/A (nonapplicable) if your child is too young for the following questions to apply:

What foods does your child like? _____

Dislike? _____

How well does your child use table utensils (cup, fork, spoon)? _____

_____

How does your child indicate bathroom needs? Word(s) for *urination:* _____

Word(s) for *bowel movement:* _____

Special words for body parts: _____

What are your child's regular bladder and bowel patterns? Do you want us to follow a particular

plan for toilet training? _____

_____

For toddlers, please describe the use of diapers or toileting equipment at home (such as a potty,

toilet seat adapter)_____

What are your child's regular sleeping patterns?

Awakes at _____ Naps at _____ Goes to bed at _____

What help does your child need to get dressed? _____

_____

Social relationships/play

What ages are your child's most frequent playmates? _____

Iş your child friendly? _____ Aggressive? _____ Shy? _____ Withdrawn? _____

Does your child play well alone? _____

What is your child's favorite toy?_____

What frightens your child? (Circle all that apply.) Animals? Rough children? Loud noises? The

dark? Storms? Anything else? _____

Who does most of the disciplining? _____

What is the best way to discipline your child? _____

_____

With which adults does your child have frequent contact? _____

How do you comfort your child? _____

Does your child use a special comforting item (such as a blanket, stuffed animal, doll)? _____

_____

Parent's signature _____

*Date*_____

Selected References

***

Books

American Academy of Pediatrics, Committee on Early Childhood, Adoption, and Dependent Care. *Health in Day Care: A Manual for Health Professionals.* Edited by S. R. Deitch, M.D. Elk Grove Village, Ill.: American Academy of Pediatrics, 1987.

American Academy of Pediatrics, Committee on Infectious Diseases. *2000 Red Book Report of the Committee on Infectious Diseases* (24th edition). Elk Grove Village, Ill.: American Academy of Pediatrics, 2000.

Berman, Christine. *Teaching Children About Food.* Palo Alto, Calif.: Bull Publishing, 1991.

Healthy Young Children: A Manual for Programs. Edited by A. S. Kendrick, R. Kaufman, and K. P. Messenger. Washington, D.C.: National Association for the Education of Young Children, 1995.

Keeping Kids Healthy: Preventing and Managing Communicable Disease in Child Care. Sacramento: California Department of Education, 1995.

Satter, Ellyn. *Child of Mine: Feeding with Love and Good Sense.* Palo Alto, Calif.: Bull Publishing, 1991.

Audiovisuals

American Academy of Pediatrics. *Caring for Our Children.* Elk Grove Village, Ill.: National Association for the Education of Young Children, 1995. Six 30-minute videocassettes.

Publications Available from the Department of Education

This publication is a component of The Program for Infant/Toddler Caregivers, a comprehensive training system for caregivers of infants and toddlers developed collaboratively by the California Department of Education and WestEd. Other available materials developed for this program include the following:

MODULE I: Social–Emotional Growth and Socialization

Videos and Video Magazines:
- First Moves: Welcoming a Child to a New Caregiving Setting
- Flexible, Fearful, or Feisty: The Different Temperaments of Infants and Toddlers
- Getting in Tune: Creating Nurturing Relationships with Infants and Toddlers

Printed Materials:
- Infant/Toddler Caregiving: A Guide to Social–Emotional Growth and Socialization
- Module I Trainer's Manual

MODULE II: Group Care

Videos and Video Magazines:
- It's Not Just Routine: Feeding, Diapering, and Napping Infants and Toddlers (Second edition)
- Respectfully Yours: Magda Gerber's Approach to Professional Infant/Toddler Care
- Space to Grow: Creating a Child Care Environment for Infants and Toddlers
- Together in Care: Meeting the Intimacy Needs of Infants and Toddlers in Groups

Printed Materials:
- Infant/Toddler Caregiving: A Guide to Routines (Second edition)
- Infant/Toddler Caregiving: A Guide to Setting Up Environments
- Module II Trainer's Manual

For more information on obtaining these materials or a free copy of the Department's *Educational Resources 2002* catalog, call CDE Press's Sales Office, 1-800-995-4099.

CDE PRESS

California Department of Education

MODULE III: Learning and Development

Videos and Video Magazines:
- The Ages of Infancy: Caring for Young, Mobile, and Older Infants
- Discoveries of Infancy: Cognitive Development and Learning
- Early Messages: Facilitating Language Development and Communication

Printed Materials:
- Infant/Toddler Caregiving: A Guide to Cognitive Development and Learning
- Infant/Toddler Caregiving: A Guide to Language Development and Communication
- Module III Trainer's Manual

MODULE IV: Culture, Family, and Providers

Videos and Video Magazines:
- Essential Connections: Ten Keys to Culturally Sensitive Child Care
- Protective Urges: Working with the Feelings of Parents and Caregivers

Printed Materials:
- Infant/Toddler Caregiving: A Guide to Creating Partnerships with Parents
- Infant/Toddler Caregiving: A Guide to Culturally Sensitive Care
- Module IV Trainer's Manual

the Program for infant toddler caregivers

Additional Materials Available in the Program

Videos and Video Magazines:
- Talking Points for Essential Connections
- Talking Points for Protective Urges
- In Our Hands
- The Next Step: Including the Infant in the Curriculum

Printed Materials:
- Addendum to Trainer's Manuals I, II, III, IV: Spanish handouts/transparencies

Module I: Social–Emotional Growth and Socialization

Title	Item no.	Quantity	Price	Total
First Moves - English video	0751		$65.00	
First Moves - Spanish video	0771		65.00	
First Moves - Chinese (Cantonese) video	0772		65.00	
First Moves - PAL English video	1416		65.00	
Flexible, Fearful, or Feisty - English video	0839		65.00	
Flexible, Fearful, or Feisty - Spanish video	0872		65.00	
Flexible, Fearful, or Feisty - Chinese (Cantonese) video	0871		65.00	
Flexible, Fearful, or Feisty - PAL English video	1417		65.00	
Getting in Tune - English video	0809		65.00	
Getting in Tune - Spanish video	0811		65.00	
Getting in Tune - Chinese (Cantonese) video	0810		65.00	
Getting in Tune - PAL English video	1418		65.00	
Infant/Toddler Caregiving: A Guide to Social–Emotional Growth and Socialization	0876		12.50	
Module I Trainer's Manual	1084		20.00	
Module I: Social–Emotional Growth and Socialization (The package price includes 3 videos, 3 accompanying video magazines, 1 curriculum guide, and 1 trainer's manual.)			**Special price**	
English videos	9928		**199.00**	
Spanish videos	9929		**199.00**	
Chinese (Cantonese) videos	9930		**199.00**	
PAL English videos	9728		**199.00**	

Module II: Group Care

Title	Item no.	Quantity	Price	Total
It's Not Just Routine - (Second edition) English video	1483		65.00	
It's Not Just Routine - (Second edition) Spanish video	1484		65.00	
It's Not Just Routine - (Second edition) Chinese (Cantonese) video	1485		65.00	
It's Not Just Routine - (Second edition) PAL English video	1506		65.00	
Respectfully Yours - English video	0753		65.00	
Respectfully Yours - Spanish video	0773		65.00	
Respectfully Yours - Chinese (Cantonese) video	0774		65.00	
Respectfully Yours - PAL English video	1422		65.00	
Space to Grow - English video	0752		65.00	
Space to Grow - Spanish video	0775		65.00	
Space to Grow - Chinese (Cantonese) video	0776		65.00	
Space to Grow - PAL English video	1423		65.00	
Together in Care - English video	1044		65.00	
Together in Care - Spanish video	0888		65.00	
Together in Care - Chinese (Cantonese) video	1051		65.00	
Together in Care - PAL English video	1424		65.00	
Infant/Toddler Caregiving: A Guide to Routines (Second edition)	1510		12.50	
Infant/Toddler Caregiving: A Guide to Setting Up Environments	0879		12.50	
Module II Trainer's Manual	1076		20.00	
Module II: Group Care (The package price includes 4 videos, 4 accompanying video magazines, 2 curriculum guides, and 1 trainer's manual.)			**Special price**	
English videos	9931		**269.00**	
Spanish videos	9932		**269.00**	
Chinese (Cantonese) videos	9933		**269.00**	
PAL English videos	9729		**269.00**	

Note: The video magazines and the curriculum guides are in English.

Module III: Learning and Development

Title	Item no.	Quantity	Price	Total
The Ages of Infancy - English video	0883		$65.00	
The Ages of Infancy - Spanish video	0884		65.00	
The Ages of Infancy - Chinese (Cantonese) video	0885		65.00	
The Ages of Infancy - PAL English video	1413		65.00	
Discoveries of Infancy - English video	1045		65.00	
Discoveries of Infancy - Spanish video	0829		65.00	
Discoveries of Infancy - Chinese (Cantonese) video	0784		65.00	
Discoveries of Infancy - PAL English video	1414		65.00	
Early Messages - English video	1425		65.00	
Early Messages - Spanish video	1446		65.00	
Early Messages - Chinese (Cantonese) video	1447		65.00	
Early Messages - PAL English video	1426		65.00	
Infant/Toddler Caregiving: A Guide to Cognitive Development and Learning	1055		12.50	
Infant/Toddler Caregiving: A Guide to Language Development and Communication	0880		12.50	
Module III Trainer's Manual	1108		20.00	
Module III: Learning and Development (The package price includes 3 videos, 3 accompanying video magazines, 2 curriculum guides, and 1 trainer's manual.)			**Special price**	
English videos	9860		**209.00**	
Spanish videos	9861		**209.00**	
Chinese (Cantonese) videos	9862		**209.00**	
PAL English videos	9730		**209.00**	

Module IV: Culture, Family, and Providers

Title	Item no.	Quantity	Price	Total
Essential Connections - English video	1056		65.00	
Essential Connections - Spanish video	1058		65.00	
Essential Connections - Chinese (Cantonese) video	1059		65.00	
Essential Connections - PAL English video	1415		65.00	
Protective Urges - English video	1270		65.00	
Protective Urges - Spanish video	1271		65.00	
Protective Urges - Chinese (Cantonese) video	1272		65.00	
Protective Urges - PAL English video	1421		65.00	
Infant/Toddler Caregiving: A Guide to Creating Partnerships with Parents	0878		12.50	
Infant/Toddler Caregiving: A Guide to Culturally Sensitive Care	1057		12.50	
Module IV Trainer's Manual	1109		20.00	
Module IV: Culture, Family, and Providers (The package price includes 2 videos, 2 accompanying video magazines, 2 curriculum guides, and 1 trainer's manual.)			**Special price**	
English videos	9774		**159.00**	
Spanish videos	9775		**159.00**	
Chinese (Cantonese) videos	9776		**159.00**	
PAL English videos	9731		**159.00**	

Additional Materials Available in The Program

Title	Item no.	Quantity	Price	Total
Talking Points for Essential Connections - English video	1370		29.00	
Talking Points for Essential Connections - PAL English video	1427		29.00	
Talking Points for Protective Urges - English video	1369		20.00	
Talking Points for Protective Urges - PAL English video	1428		20.00	
Talking Points for Essential Connections - 50 video magazines (English)	9744		17.50	
Talking Points for Protective Urges - 50 video magazines (English)	9743		17.50	
Addendum to Trainer's Manuals I, II, III, IV: Spanish handouts/transparencies	1395		20.00	
In Our Hands - English video	1432		19.00	
In Our Hands - PAL English video	1419		19.00	
In Our Hands - 50 video magazines (English)	9747		17.50	

Video Magazines

Title	Item no.	Quantity	Price	Total
The Ages of Infancy - 50 video magazines (English)	9954		$17.50	
The Ages of Infancy - 50 video magazines (Spanish)	9732		17.50	
Discoveries of Infancy - 50 video magazines (English)	9974		17.50	
Discoveries of Infancy - 50 video magazines (Spanish)	9733		17.50	
Early Messages - 50 video magazines (English)	9747		17.50	
Early Messages - 50 video magazines (Spanish)	9734		17.50	
Essential Connections - 50 video magazines (English)	9869		17.50	
Essential Connections - 50 video magazines (Spanish)	9735		17.50	
First Moves - 50 video magazines (English)	9960		17.50	
First Moves - 50 video magazines (Spanish)	9736		17.50	
Flexible, Fearful, or Feisty - 50 video magazines (English)	9956		17.50	
Flexible, Fearful, or Feisty - 50 video magazines (Spanish)	9737		17.50	
Getting in Tune - 50 video magazines (English)	9957		17.50	
Getting in Tune - 50 video magazines (Spanish)	9738		17.50	
It's Not Just Routine - 50 video magazines (Second edition) (English)	9724		17.50	
It's Not Just Routine - 50 video magazines (Second edition) (Spanish)	9723		17.50	
Protective Urges - 50 video magazines (English)	9778		17.50	
Protective Urges - 50 video magazines (Spanish)	9739		17.50	
Respectfully Yours - 50 video magazines (English)	9958		17.50	
Respectfully Yours - 50 video magazines (Spanish)	9740		17.50	
Space to Grow - 50 video magazines (English)	9959		17.50	
Space to Grow - 50 video magazines (Spanish)	9741		17.50	
Together in Care - 50 video magazines (English)	9873		17.50	
Together in Care - 50 video magazines (Spanish)	9742		17.50	
Sampler pack of 3 video magazines for each video in Modules I, II, III, and IV (available) (English)	9720		17.50	
Sampler pack of 3 video magazines for each video in Modules I, II, III, and IV (Spanish)	9719		17.50	

ORDER FORM

Mail orders should be directed to:

California Department of Education
CDE Press, Sales Office
P.O. Box 271
Sacramento, CA
95812-0271

FAX: 916-323-0823

For credit-card orders:
Call the Sales Office at
1-800-995-4099.

SHIPPING AND HANDLING   UPS REQUIRES A STREET ADDRESS.

All orders to be delivered within the continental U.S. are shipped via United Parcel Service (UPS), ground ONLY. Orders to HAWAII and ALASKA are shipped via UPS Second Day Air. An additional charge for the actual shipping cost plus a handling fee will be added to your credit card order. For international orders, contact CDE Press for estimate of shipping costs.

Shipping and Handling Charges

Number of copies	Add	Number of copies	Add	Number of copies	Add	Number of copies	Add
1	$5.95	9–12	$14.95	21–24	$19.95	33–36	$26.95
2–4	7.95	13–16	15.95	25–28	21.95	37–40	28.95
5–8	9.95	17–20	17.95	29–32	23.95	40+ call 1-800-995-4099	

Note: Shipping and handling charges for Modules are $5.95 for each Module.

Subtotal	$
California residents add sales tax.	
Shipping and handling charges (See chart.)	
TOTAL AMOUNT	$

Note: Mail orders must be accompanied by a check or a purchase order. For VISA or MasterCard purchases, call the toll-free number 1-800-995-4099. Purchase orders without checks are accepted from educational institutions, businesses, and governmental agencies. Stated prices are subject to change. Please order carefully; include correct item number and quantity for each item ordered. *All sales are final.*

Name _____

Agency _____

Shipping address _____

City _____ State _____ ZIP code _____

the Program for infant toddler caregivers

99-025 102-2854-156 4-02 5M